I0140837

Rev. Bil
Unplugged & Unedited

ॐ ॐ ॐ

MetaSpiritual Truths that Challenge
Unquestioned Answers So You Can
Master the Art of Living in Skin School
by Walking the Spirtual Path on Practical Feet

Rev. Bil Holton, Ph.D.

© 2017 The Global Center For Spiritual Awakening

Copyright ©2017 Bil Holton

All rights reserved.

Reproduction or translation of any part of this work beyond that permitted by Section 107 or 108 of the 1976 United States Copyright Act without the permission of the copyright owner is unlawful. Requests for permission or further information should be addressed to the authors, c/o Prosperity Publishing House, 1405 Autumn Ridge Drive, Durham. NC 27712.

This publication is designed to provide accurate and authoritative information in regard to the subject matter covered. It is sold with the understanding that the publisher is not engaged in rendering legal, accounting, or other professional service. If legal advice or other expert assistance is required, the services of a competent professional person should be sought. *From a Declaration of Principles jointly adopted by a Committee of the American Bar Association and a Committee of Publishers.*

Prosperity Publishing House
Durham, NC

Library of Congress Cataloging-in-Publication Data

Holton, Bil
Rev. Bil Unplugged and Unedited / Bil Holton
         p. cm.
      Includes bibliographical references.
      ISBN 978-1-893095-86-1
      1. Spiritual   2. New Thought   3. Self Help
      II. Title

Library of Congress Control Number: 2017937964
Printed in the United States of America

10 9 8 7 6 5 4 3 2 1

Table of Contents

Introduction

I've written this book for people who consider themselves more spiritual than religious, who recognize that their True Essence is divine, who have outgrown the need to worship a god 'out there' who punishes 'sinners' and keeps the faithful fearful and petitioning for the things they want. The content in this book is very definitely for people who are open-minded in matters that are spiritual, metaphysical, allegorical, metaphorical, scientific and spiritual.

I elaborate just a bit more on the term MetaSpirituality, which Cher and I coined to describe the ceilingless marriage between spirituality, metaphysics, quantum physics, philosophy, neuroscience, biology, Theosophy, Rosicrucian teachings, anthroposophy, gnostic teachings, genetics and epigenetics, positive psychology, Enochian teachings, epistemology and cosmology, the esoteric teachings of the world's major faith traditions, etc., and the spiritual insights gained from our own spiritual practices. (See our books entitled *Straight Talk About Spiritual Stuff* and *More Straight Talk About Spiritual Stuff*)

MetaSpirituality is a way of life. It invites you to 'leave your nets.' 'Leaving your nets' means subordinating your material interests to your spiritual growth. It means choosing to live at the speed of your enlightenment, so your Divine Nature can 'net' you the Self-Realization you seek as you strive for aligning (oneing) your human nature with your *Higher Spiritual Nature*.

It's the ceilinglessness, limitlessness and expansiveness of MetaSpirituality that interests Cher and I, and which we believe will interest you, too. It frees you to challenge all unquestioned answers in order to gain a broader realization of, and deepen your understanding of, your place in the universe. And as you gain new insights you'll feel a sense of awe and giddiness that tells you that you're on to something extraordinary.

With God (Pure Universal Consciousness, One Reality, Infinite Isness, Eternal Presence) expressing Itself through Its *Logos* Nature in human form as you, you'll be able to disentangle yourself from your small 's' self (human self) by aligning (oneing) yourself with your capital 'S' *Self (Higher Spiritual Self)*. That means you must not repress your *Higher Spiritual Self*. Once you maintain a tight alignment (oneing) with your *Logos Nature,* you'll attract the Universal Truth Principles you need to guarantee your eventual illumination and Self-Realization. And that illumination—your Self-Realization—can be just a thought, an insight, an intuition away. It's a state of higher consciousness that you can achieve in this lifetime!

If you're like us, you've outgrown the dogmatic mindset of mainstream Christianity. Mainstream Christianity, including religious fundamentalism, is built on the belief of humankind's alienation from an anthropomorphic god meme in the sky who is separate from us. And this 'alienation complex' has birthed an atonement theology that reflects humankind's supposed 'fall from grace.' We prefer an 'at-one-ment' spiritual perspective that focuses on our *worthship* as spiritual beings having a human experience and affirms our oneness as indivisible human extensions of the One Reality (Pure Universal Consciousness, Infinite Isness, Eternal Presence).

You'll find that my 'unplugged tone' in this book calls for the dismissal of the concept of a vengeful, amygdala-driven, anthropomorphic god in the sky. I advocate 'defriending' dogma and disowning a literal-only interpretation of sacred scripture. I propose growing beyond the embedded religious theology of your youth—in order to open your mind to the perennial wisdom and universal truths that reveal your True Divine Nature!

For example, in quantum physics terms, 'cosmic inflation' is the idea that, in the first split-second after the Big Bang, the universe underwent a fantastically fast (exponential) expansion driven by the vacuum of space. When it comes to spiritual growth, the same thing happens when you are introduced to a new MetaSpiritual teaching (Big Bang) that causes your awareness to expand exponentially into inner space (your thought universe).

You'll find throughout the pages of this book that I invite you to use a multiplicity of religious practices and turn them into spiritual practices. I prescribe what I call 'spiritual inoculations' to help you build a solid spiritual practice. Here are some Cher and I use to inoculate ourselves from the world of outer appearances: meditation; affirmative prayer; spiritual visualizations; positive affirmations and resolute denials; the support of like-minded friends and family; a positive attitude; an optimistic spirit; a giving consciousness; affirming your alignment (oneing) with your innate divinity; and disciplined metaphysical study.

Your devotion to disciplined spiritual practice will produce in you a *Self Conscious* rhythm that will become so powerful that all unlike energies and vibrations are eliminated. The blight of error thoughts (kamikaze or intentional), egocentric choices and discordant actions will no longer contaminate your consciousness. Divinely alchemicalized currents will flow through every cell, atom and molecule of your physical, emotional and mental body making you a highly spiritualized container of divine audacity.

There's one more thing you should know about my MetaSpiritual focus: MetaSpirituality generally interferes with dogmatic biases, denominational sparring, religious exclusivity, mainstream churches' science phobia, and the denigration of women and same sex couples.

Welcome to the unplugged Rev. Bil, and I humbly invite you to allow what you read in these pages as teases to deepen and expand your own appreciation for your own innate wisdom as you continue your journey toward your own Self-Realization.

By the way, if you haven't come across it yet, check out our online ministry, The Global Center for Spiritual Awakening.com—our cyber spiritual IP address, and hopefully your soon-to-be adopted cyber spiritual home!

Namaste.

ॐ   ॐ   ॐ

Abracadabra-ing

Abracadabra-ing is using mindfulness meditation, affirmative prayer, visualization, open-mindedness, optimism, intuitiveness, mysticism, transcendentalness, metaphysical and esoteric teachings, and positive affirmations as the open sesames to happiness, healing and enlightenment.

Acceptance

Stop questioning the validity of your existence. If you weren't here, there would be a lot of other people, places and things that wouldn't be here.

Accepting things as they *are* is not the same thing as accepting things as they *come*.

Acupuncture

What if hugs, smiles, playful eye winks, compliments, kisses on the cheek, holding hands, rest, a soothing sip of hot coffee or tea, and mutual sharing of highly personal information are all forms of spiritual acupuncture!

Adamic Arsenic

The unenlightened ego is a form of Adamic arsenic. It is poisonous (arsenic) to your spiritual growth. The instability you feel when you refuse to acknowledge your Divine Core is the plight of an unenlightened ego. In a very real sense, an unenlightened ego is the antithesis of spiritual growth. An anti-spiritual growth mentality sees separation, breeds separation, and leads to a life of unnecessary isolation from your Higher Spiritual Self and literally cultivates a propensity toward darkness and despair. What makes your recalcitrant ego especially paranoid at any level of your spiritual development is that it realizes it must be totally subordinated (become totally selfless and accepting) by being absorbed into your Deeper Self (Divine Nature or Higher Spiritual Self) if you are to become a fully illuminated being.

Adept

MetaSpiritually speaking, an adept is a highly evolved spiritual idea, sacred spiritual principle or divine insight. It also refers to a highly enlightened, spiritually-attuned human being, or other intelligent highly conscious being, who has mastered his or her skin school, dimensional, interdimensional and/or intra-dimensional experiences.

Affirmations

There's so much news out there now to depress us if we allow it, and create fear in our lives if we permit it! I reach out to you and boldly say: Do not give into anything that's the product of outer appearances! Face life with joy. Do it with every thought, each choice and every action. For example, when you wake up and feel grouchy, immediately affirm, "I greet this day with joy!" When you have to do some project that you're not looking forward to, simply affirm, "I do this with joy!" You'll be amazed at the difference. A great denial / affirmation is this: "No one or no thing can rob me of my joy! I face life with joy!" (A denial is an assertion that gives no power to outer appearances).

Affirmations are powerful, purposeful intentions to align (entrain) your human self with your Divine Nature (Cosmic Logos Nature) so you can achieve what you desire by right of consciousness as you move toward (unfold into) Self-Realization (become consciously one with your Logos Nature).

Say your affirmations like you mean them … like you *believe* them! Affirm them with conviction! [*Finish this sentence: It's not only WHAT you say, it's* …] Put your zeal and energy behind the words! And then become aware of the energy boost you feel as you affirm the truth of who you really are, and notice the change you experience in your ability to bring a sense of well-thought-out, sensible order – Divinely Ordering Your Good – to whatever you are doing. If you're not doing that, you're kidding yourself if you expect to get traction in your spiritual growth. I'm not kidding about that. You'll get the traction you need, because you're worth getting the traction you need! (See the TH Factor and *Worthship* references.)

Affirmative Prayer

Pleasant thoughts, positive and optimistic inclinations, sitting meditations, and affirmative prayers are all dopamine triggers. Dopamine, the pleasure chemical, is produced when we see the world as a safe, life-enriching experience.

Make each affirmative prayer a doxology toward your health, wealth, happiness and Self-Realization. By the way, affirmative prayers are just a series of positive affirmations that you employ to underwrite your greater good.

Pray affirmatively for twelve minutes and exercise for twenty-one minutes today, unless you're too tired or too busy. In that case, double the time for each activity. Why? Because if you haven't done the '12-to-21' ritual today, your 'material lacticity' will slow both your spiritual practice and your happiness down.

Ahylozoics

Ahylozoics is a mouthful, isn't it? It's a term I've coined which means that all matter (including dark matter and dark energy) in the physical universe is a product of the Apeiron nature of Pure Universal Consciousness (the One Reality). (See the *Cosmic Logos* and Word references in this book and the Apeiron reference in our *More Straight Talk About Spiritual Stuff* book for a more detailed look.)

Akashic Records

The Akashic Records are believed to be an experiential body of timeless knowledge that contains the energetic signatures of the origin of sentient souls, previous lifetimes, soul intentions and purposes, and future points of choice and possibility. With billions of choices, thoughts and actions made by billions of people each-consecutive-moment-of-now throughout humankind's presence on earth – and our presence as spiritual beings in other dimensions - the Akashic Records change and are updated every nano-second.

The total information about you (your Book of Life, *Quantum Self*) includes many incarnations and reincarnations on the earth plane and in other dimensions of being. So, the information you seek will come in bytes and bits, a little at a time. (See the Book of Life, Consciousness, Dweller on the Threshold, Lower Four Bodies, Noah's Ark, Soul Spelunking, and Xenoglossia references)

The Akashic Records are reported to be the collective brain dump, aggregate emotional energy and cumulative psychical prodigiousness of all of the sentient beings who have stepped into our universe.

Alpha and Omega

The world is your 'inn' and your physical body is your 'manger' in an incarnational experience. Out of your quantum beginning (Alpha Point) you have an opportunity to grow into an awareness of your Divine Nature. Once you attain that higher awareness of your divine stature by upping your consciousness, you can transform your earthly body (and any of your extra-dimensional bodies) into a highly alchemicalized vehicle of consciousness (Omega Point) and free yourself from the confines and limitations of physicality. The irony is captured by T.S. Eliot in *Little Gidding*: "And the end of all our exploring will be to arrive where we started. And know the place for the first time." And, I believe that place is the '*Higher Self-Centric You*' which is your True Spiritual Nature.

A-Musing

I love to live in the lateral, out-of-the-box thinking world, because there's a lot more room 'out there.' And that's the only place (state of consciousness) you're going to find the Muse who loves plenty of elbow room, too.

Angels

Adepts, ascended beings, celestial guides, divine messengers, supernatural beings, spiritual Samaritans, ascended spiritual masters, benevolent immortals, and advanced spiritual teachers can all be referred to as angels. They are Self-Realized spiritual beings who have mastered the human experience (and other interdimensional experiences) and make themselves available to guide and assist highly conscious beings who are not as advanced spiritually. One day you, too, shall become 'angelic' and either help sentient beings on earth and/or in other dimensions.

Antahkarana Bridge

The *antahkarana* bridge (rainbow bridge, divine corridor, spinal column) describes the pathway of your entry into higher consciousness. This cosmic bridge (not to be confused with the beautifully written pet rainbow bridge) is built with the intent and mental substance of concentrated focus through many lifetimes. The quality of that focus becomes more refined as you achieve greater levels of Self-Realization.

Anthropomorphic God Meme

In my opinion, mainstream religious traditions worship an anthropomorphic God meme. A meme, as you know, is an idea, a belief, catch phrase, or pattern of behavior that goes viral and spreads throughout a culture like a virus. It's a self-replicating theme that's transmitted mindlessly from one person to another through written and spoken words, gestures, rituals, news and social media.

For example, the phrases 'the good die young,' fake it 'till you make it,' and 'I didn't have a choice' are social memes. Santa Claus, the Easter Bunny, the Tooth Fairy and Mr. Clean are marketing memes—to name a very, very, very few of the thousands of memes. Memes are especially contagious to those who are highly impressionable and neglect to question unquestioned answers. Dogmatic religious beliefs are memes and infect tens of millions of people.

In the principles of unity, non-locality, and holographic wholeness which physicists, neuroscientists, and metaphysicians have set forth, you are not the creation of an anthropomorphic, white-bearded, white-clothed God meme in the sky, who molded and shaped you and set you on the path of life 'down here' in skin school. I believe humankind got that notion from a super-powerful being (avatar, extraterrestrial, extremely adept spiritual teacher, etc.) who came to earth from another dimension eons ago and appeared godlike, because he had abilities that humankind had never seen before (agelessness, bilocation/multilocation, far superior intellect and mental power, psychic powers, telepathy, immense physical strength, levitation, disappearing and re-appearing abilities, etc. (I said 'he' because all of the god meme images are masculine).

Humankind mistook that super being as the Creator of the Universe and our collective consciousness bought into that 'creator god meme, which went viral. Here's something else I believe and it's the foundation of all of my subsequent MetaSpiritual beliefs: You are, we are—humankind is—the physical presence (localized actualization) of the Ultimate Reality (Pure Universal Consciousness, One Reality, etc.) expressing Itself as us. (See MetaSpirituality reference).

Anti-Semantic

When people tell me I'm playing *semantics* (the branch of linguistics and logic concerned with meaning) when it comes to my penchant for updating the language I use to describe Cher's and my amped-up MetaSpiritual teachings, I generally respond that we're not *anti-semantic*! I invent language all of the time in order to clarify our MetaSpiritual and metaphysical teachings.

Here are a few of our favorite *semantics*: Internal Lotus of Control, insperiences, abracadabra-ing, authentegrity, cellular theology, chatter bombs, fundies (religious fundamentalists), dogmatic carcasses, duhology, errornami, formaldehyde beliefs, gourmet gospel, immaculate reception, intention deficit disorder, irritable vowel syndrome, karmic sludge, literalbots, low-voltage congregants, mental shampoo, metaphysical aikido, neocortex moments, one-channel religion, optical delusions, ouijing around, scarecrowology, sinnami, soul spelunking, spiritual emojis, spiritual URL, spiritual IP address, thought pharmacy, uppity nincompoop, etc. Wasn't that a fun snippet! Hope you're leaning toward not being *anti-semantic* too!

Anti-Semitism

According to the traditional interpretation of the Biblical account, when Pilate released Barabbas instead of Jesus, and then turned Jesus over to the crowd by ceremoniously washing his own hands, claiming "I am innocent of this man's blood. It is your responsibility," the crowd responded by shouting, "Let his blood be on us and on our children" (Matthew 27:24-25).

I believe those words "Let his blood be on us ..." have been used for centuries to justify the horrors of anti-Semitism. MetaSpiritually, I believe this is what these two verses mean: 24. When the mortal mind (Pilate) senses that an interior spiritual transformation is at hand, we resist any change that might undermine our materialistic biases (our Barabbas tendencies) and refuse to embrace the soul-deepening implications of that transformation and so we neglect to take responsibility (Pilate washes his hands) for working toward our eventual Self-Realization (our capital 'S' *Self - Higher Spiritual Self, Logos-Self, Fully-Enlightened Self*). 25. All of our riotous, unredeemed, mortal thoughts and encrusted patterns of error (the unenlightened throng of people) prompt us to declare our avowed attachment to sense appetites (His blood be on us...) and reinforce our resistance to actualizing our Divine Nature.

The whole scene I've just described in those two verses is humankind's archetypical reaction for refusing to align our human self with our Higher Spiritual Nature. It's time we stopped blaming someone and something else for our own poor choices, especially our penchant for denying our own innate divinity and the innate divinity in others! And it's certainly time for us to stop using Jewish people as scapegoats for humankind's divinity-denying error prone nature and for their 'role' in an allegorical New Testament story.

Apparitions

I believe the majority of reported apparitions that can't be explained medically (extremely high body temperature, administered synthetic narcotic drugs such as morphine and Demerol that produce hallucinogenic reactions, and psychoactive agents that cause perceptual anomalies and psychoses) may very well be karmic anomalies that arise from the interdimensional consciousness dynamics which the other versions of us experience since we are still connected psychically with those versions of us. There are also cosmic entanglements (interconnectiveness, nonlocal dynamics) that come into play due to the nonlocality of consciousness.

Apocalypse

The interesting thing about humankind's collective doomsday thinking, in my opinion, is that it's based on a hidden truth that's been corrupted by the genealogical guilt trip we've laid on ourselves since the beginning of our time on Earth! We've perpetuated it by concocting apocalyptic scenarios and producing movies that glamorize the end of the human race ad nauseam.

The good news is, there will be no, nor has there ever been a 'God-ordained' mass extinction of the human race! (You may want to read that sentence again, because there's no white-bearded, white-robed anthropomorphic god meme in the sky that does that sort of thing)! That kind of global apocalypse is a figment of our collective imaginations. That's not to say there couldn't be an anthropogenic extinction. We humans have been known to make a few poor choices throughout our skin school history.

The apocalyptic 'restoration' I predict will be humankind growing spiritually enough and enlightened enough to outgrow our egocentric worldly nature by remembering who we really are and becoming *Self-Realized* enough that we grow fully into and express our Divine Nature which has always been our birthright. It will be the end of the unenlightened ego's temporal rulership and the beginning of our Divine Nature's full expression. Peace will be established on earth (our unenlightened egocentric consciousness) like it is in heaven (our fully illuminated super-consciousness).

Apocalyptic Awareness

To continue to believe in a literalistic view of sacred scripture and not know that it is a corrosive, limited perspective, perpetuates apocalyptic global suffering. It's one of the most debilitating forms of mainstream religious practice.

A literal interpretation of scripture is like carbon monoxide—it's pathological nature is undetectable and can poison the sensitivities of literabots who can't stomach the truth, get dizzy when they are forced outside of their dogmatic boxes, or suffer from headaches whenever they come across MetaSpiritual teachings.

Ark of the Covenant

The Ark of the Covenant is an age old religious artifact that means different things to different people. For some, the Ark is a mystical object that contains supernatural powers too terrifying to comprehend. For movie goers, it's the priceless treasure sought after by the fearless Indiana Jones in *Raiders of the Lost Ark*. To others, it's an ancient treasure that's highly coveted for its 'religious' significance. Taking into account all of the enticing myths surrounding the mysterious Ark, it's worthwhile to take a moment to give you a MetaSpiritual perspective which takes all of the characteristics associated with the literal Ark and uses them as metaphors for the thoughts, feelings, talents, skills and inclinations that are within us.

The conventional stories about the Ark of the Covenant (also called the 'ark of the Lord,' 'ark of God,' 'ark of the covenant of the Lord' and 'ark of the testimony') generally allude to three items of extreme significance to the Israelites. The first was two stone tablets bearing the divine inscription of the Ten Commandments which formed the foundation of the Jewish God's covenant with Israel. The second major item believed to have been in the Ark was the rod of Aaron. According to Jewish tradition, their God miraculously caused Aaron's rod to bud with blossoms to legitimize Aaron's being in charge of the Priesthood. The last 'treasure' was a golden pot of manna. According to the literal interpretation, manna was the starchy food their God miraculously provided for the Israelites during their 40 years of wandering in the wilderness.

The Ark was carried ahead of the Israelites wherever they traveled. Not only was it the centerpiece of worship when it was placed in the tabernacle, but its supernatural powers protected the Israelites in battle by defeating their adversaries.

Literalistic accounts bear the mark of folk-stories and contribute to the supernatural accounts of the Ark as having an other-worldly origin. However, in my opinion, although there are many theories of what the mysterious Ark of the Covenant was and what its purpose was, you'll find a very interesting perspective of both the Arks (Ark of Covenant and Noah's Ark) in a MetaSpiritual interpretation, which doesn't support its material (physical) form at all.

From a MetaSpiritual perspective our super-consciousness is the upper deck of the fabled Noah's Ark. Our physical body is the lower deck of the Ark! That makes the integration of our human consciousness and our Higher Spiritual Consciousness necessary for *Self Realization*. The two Cherubim (one on the right and the other on the left) that faced each other on top of the golden lid cover on the Ark of the Covenant represent our spiritualized left and right brain hemispheres respectively. The construction of both Arks is a symbol for the dynamic mental processes and psychic abilities that characterize our super-consciousness development.

Because we are born with two brain hemispheres that see the world in two different ways, this account clearly suggests that we have evolved the wherewithal to integrate both hemispheres to conceive a unified whole. MetaSpiritually, the pairs of animals that went into Noah's Ark represent the various polarities that make up our mental, physical and emotional bodies (positive/negative thoughts; right/left brain hemispheres; love/fear; sadness/happiness; ill will/goodwill; mindfulness/mindlessness; etc.). The pairs of animals could also refer to the two channels (ida and pingala) associated with the kundalini's rise through our chakras which are energy centers along the spinal column. We enter into the Sacred 72 Centimeter path (our spinal cord) every time we elevate our thinking, being and doing to a spiritual octave. The 72 centimeter path is called by the Hindus the 'razor-edged path' and by the Buddhists the 'Noble Eightfold Path.' (See the Straight Is the Gate and Narrow Is the Way reference in this book and the 72 Centimeter reference in our book entitled *More Straight Talk About Spiritual Stuff.)*

Ascension

At some point in our spiritual unfoldment we will not need a physical form as we Self-Realize into more suitable vibratory 'quarters.' The closer we get to Self-Realization the less need we'll have for a 'leased somatic vehicle.'

Attachments

Attachments are ornamental reactions to something we feel we need to complete us. They are prompted by an unenlightened ego which wants to surround itself with materialistic things and addictive sensory appetites.

Authentegrity

If you don't believe in it, authentegrity won't come out of your mouth, body language, promises, choices or actions.

We should all be more authentic than some of our smarts.

You can stand firm, stand tall and stand anything as long as you can stand yourself.

Generally speaking, where you stand usually depends on what you'll fall for.

Professed adherence to spiritual principles that is clearly articulated, but not honored, is like writing on water.

Awakened Doing

Awakened doing is the kind of mindfulness that will bring you enlightenment. Consciously aligning (entraining) your humanness with your spiritualness is awakened doing.

Awakened being, awakened doing and awakened having constitute the mindfulness trinity that will set you free from the centrifugal force of materialism.

ॐ   ॐ   ॐ

Babymoon

MetaSpiritually speaking, I refer to the period of time when neophytes enjoy basic esoteric teachings before they are introduced to more advanced teachings as a babymoon. (In social networking, a babymoon is a relaxing or romantic holiday taken by parents-to-be before their baby is born).

Badware

Bad habits and divinity-denying thoughts and actions (badware) ultimately lead to soul decay. They're tough to unravel and criticism about them usually leads to ill feelings and defensiveness. If you've ever tried to untangle a piece of string, you know that yanking on it or pulling too hard only makes unraveling it more difficult. Sometimes you can untie it with your fingers. Other times you have to use a sharp object to pry between the folds of the knot to loosen it. Occasionally cutting the knot is the only thing that works. The point is, the more entangled something is, the more effort it takes to free it from itself.

Freeing yourself from self-defeating thoughts and Self-negating habits (badware—and then staying free—may mean cutting yourself free before you use the same bad habit in the next crisis. Re-using habits that don't work is a yarn you need to unravel quickly and permanently.

When your bad habits zig at you today, zag.

Barbaric Theology

What humankind needs is not a barbaric religious theology of denigration, ridicule and defamation. What we need is a spiritual perspective that affirms our oneness with the Pure Universal Consciousness which is the Ground of All Being – and Non-being.

Beliefs

Did you know that living too high in the clouds can make you light-headed? Bringing lofty beliefs down to earth in a way they can be used – and understood—is what makes them valuable and believable. Timing is important. Beliefs and values need clear runways and plenty of landing room. Otherwise your landing field will be cluttered with ideals, values and beliefs that crash and burn.

In order to grow spiritually you must leave formaldehyde beliefs and fossilized dogmas behind. You must be ready for a thought triage, a new calculus of belief, when you encounter an expanded perspective that's totally outside of your current conceptual and experiential bandwidth.

If your professed beliefs aren't being translated into action, I invite you to give yourself a mental shampoo, followed up with conditioners like the spiritual practices you'll find on our website, in our webinars, and during our highly popular spiritual cafés.

Beliefs are ego-generated filters that can cloud our perceptions and color our experience. We manufacture them to make sense out of our skin school experience.

One of the dangers of owning certain beliefs and professing particular values is that you have many opportunities to prove them by your actions. If you're un-true to your beliefs or fail to do what it takes to honor your beliefs, it's the same as not having that belief at all. You've heard the expression "faith without works is dead." The same thing applies to beliefs, no matter how lofty or noble they are. Beliefs without complementary choices and actions are only professed beliefs.

Biblical Literalism

Biblical literalism is the mindless weapon of choice of religious fundamentalists who use their scriptural literality to spread their poisonous hatred, vicious hurtfulness, and malicious cruelty in pandemic proportions to anyone who disagrees with their addiction to a literal interpretation of Biblical scripture.

Biblical literalism is dogma gone mad!

Historically, the Jewish people were held in captivity by the Assyrians, the Babylonians, and the Egyptians. And now the New Testament stories by Jewish writers 2,000 years ago are being held hostage by the fanatical literalism of what I call the 'Christian literalist captivity!'

Biblical literalism leaves you hanging in uncomfortable ecumenical space.

A scientist at Harvard Medical School, found that there's a mechanism in our cells that can recognize when things are going on and prevent cancer from breaking out. The mechanism is called 'DNA damage response' and it works like an intelligence agent that monitors when things go awry, and finds a way to deal with them. It's key to our body's ability to prevent diseases as we continue to age. MetaSpiritually speaking, when we outgrow our cancerous religious dogmatism and Biblical literalist biases, we sort of develop a 'Biblical literalism damage control response' that prevents damage to our spiritual growth. I'm just say'in.

I'm not allergic to Biblical literalism; however, I must confess, I take a metaphysical pill to strengthen my immune system whenever I read literalist scripture or am around people who read or recite it.

Literalist Bible studies tend to learn less and less about more and more. Covering the content in all sixty-six books from a literal-only perspective is more or less an exercise in what I call 'one channel' redundancy. If the only 'interpretive channel' is literalism, the hidden wisdom (*vidya*) in the scriptures never rises to the surface. If you don't dig deeper, all you're doing is hydroplaning. And if you've ever hydroplaned, the skid generally takes you somewhere you'd rather not go.

What's appealing to Biblical literalists is usually appalling to metaphysicians.

Stop trying to duct-tape your spiritual growth by interpreting all Biblical scripture literally.

The bizarre stories that characterize many literal interpretations of Biblical scripture, as well as the exoteric myths of a number of other faith traditions are carnival fun house and horror house distortions of reality. I believe you'd better serve your spiritual growth and human happiness if you would interpret them as archetypical renditions of spiritual growth themes that have important metaphysical implications for human beings in general.

Biblical Literalist Memories Questioned

A frontal assault on Biblical literalism won't work, because volatile emotions always trump reason, common sense and facts.

According to psychologists there are three types of personal memories: episodic, semantic and procedural. The third kind, procedural, involves remembering to do things with your body like: how to breathe using meditation breathing techniques, how to hit a sand wedge, how to use a fitness tracker app, etc. I invite you to research this type of memory, but I'm not going to cover it for the purposes of this reference, because it has little relevance regarding the historical accuracy of the gospels and what they tell us about the historical Yeshua (Jesus).

However, the other two types of memory are relevant:

- Episodic memory is the kind of memory that allows you to recall things that actually happened to you personally, like: who was the recipient of your first kiss, where you went to high school and/or college, what your favorite frozen custard is, etc.
- Semantic memory involves factual information about things that you haven't personally witnessed, but know to be true, like: Duke won the NCAA basketball championship in 2015, Tiger Woods has won the Masters Golf Championship four times (1997, 2001, 2002, 2005), the Eiffel Tower is 1,063 feet tall, spider silk is used in bone repair, etc.

The fact is, all of us misremembers things in our past and even distorts factual information from time-to-time. You agree with that, right? Okay. In addition to the three personal memory categories, there's such a thing as what sociologists call 'collective memory,' which refers to how social and cultural groups remember past people, places, things and events. All four of these types of memory come into play to produce stories of Yeshua's (Jesus') life and teachings that are believed to be true or distortions of the truth, fact or fiction, doubtless or invented, authentic or apocryphal, etc.

Literalism is religious fundamentalism gone berserk! It overlooks common sense and sound judgment, discounts metaphysical and allegorical truths, represses and denies universal archetypical patterns, and has a phobic reaction to scientific evidence. If I wasn't concerned about the length of this book, I'd really tell you how I feel about over-cooked Biblical literalism!

If you haven't researched it, there's a coterie of non-canonical books and gospels about Yeshua (Jesus) written before the synoptic gospels that are filled with some rather interesting—and even bizarre—eyewitness, second-hand, third-hand … tenth-hand, and widely circulated 'memories' about his life and teachings. Some of the most researched are: the Gospel of Peter, the Acts of Peter, the Coptic Gospel of Thomas, the Infancy Gospel of Thomas, the Proto-Gospel of James, the Gospel of Pseudo-Matthew, the Gospel of Nicodemus, the Correspondence With Abgar, the Acts of Pilate, the Letter of Pilate to Herod, the Report of Pilate, the Expositions of the Sayings of the Lord. These 'memories'—as well as false memories—do not seem to be based on, or related to, Jewish liturgy. What's really interesting—and telling—is that credible research has found that eyewitness accounts are notoriously inaccurate and unreliable AND 'group memory' tends to be even less reliable.

Literalism remains a sad inheritance for those who grow up in mainstream Christianity.

One of the saddest things about Biblical literalism is that it neuroticizes the faithful and brainwashes them into plunging headlong into a sort of collective hysteria.

According to highly credible research, it's often difficult to determine what we have actually witnessed and what commonsense tells us happened. As incredible as it sounds, commonsense , along with the details about someone or something we receive via hearsay from friends and people we don't know 'conspire' in distorting—and even fabricating—legitimate memories. The only writings we have about Yeshua (Jesus) between age 12 and 30 are non-canonical. They were not included in the canon – and quite frankly, for good reason. Some of the 'memories' are outlandish! The same 'memory leakage' occurs in every faith tradition when stories about its founder(s) and well-known followers are recollected.

According to highly reliable research (hope you're not getting tired of the research I'm tossing at you), people—even people who grew up in word-of-mouth cultures—'remember' all sorts of things (some of them in evocative, vividly fascinating detail), even though what they 'remembered' never happened! The power of suggestion, colorful storytelling, and the influence of an authority figure who is telling the story, more often than not can generate an 'alternate reality.'

Both real and fabricated events, if repeated often enough, can become part of the hearer's enduring memory. In the case of the stories about Jesus, we know that the word-of-mouth reliability and unreliability of eyewitness reports are suspect, and, if you add to that, the confusion that the editing, interpretation, translation, transliteration, and liturgical treatments have on the reliability of the written account, you can appreciate the concerns I – and a coterie of truth-seeking metaphysicians and Biblical scholars – have about the historicity and myths surrounding Jesus (Yeshua) of Nazareth and other religious luminaries.

One of the problems with eyewitness accounts is that they're all 'I' witness accounts.

Outside of the cushioned pews of conservative, evangelical and fundamental Christians, very few, if any, Bible scholars, or highly discerning people in the general populace, believe that all of the reported stories about Jesus—and in the Bible as a whole—are accurate and reliable. As credible research has shown, eyewitness accounts are not necessarily the guarantors of 'source reliability.'

Literalists who defend the oral tradition rarely let facts get in the way of their opinions. For example, they claim that people who grow up in oral cultures (non-literary cultures) have more reliable memories because they have to remember what was said and who did what. They tout that accurate memories and total recall are in their 'DNA' in order for them to past down their shared history by word of mouth without changing a thing or missing anything that happened. However, the research says that people in oral cultures —which would have been Yeshua's (Jesus' era)—generally forget as much as people in literary cultures, or any other culture. In many instances they tend to be less accurate, because oral cultures have no way of checking the accuracy (chain of transmission) of their stories over time, and particularly over long spans of time.

In oral traditions, the recall of historical happenings depends on how accurate that recall is, and the recall of the people who hear the storyteller's story depends on the quality and accuracy of their recall—and so on, for as long as the story is told. How much is factual and how much is just a mirage (interpretive gymnastics) as the chain of transmission unfolds year after year? I'm just say'in!

Biblicist Babel

Some biblicists argue that Biblical chronology fixes the date of the Earth's creation at 4004 BCE. That suggests that the earth is a little over six thousand years old. Present-day creationists stubbornly believe in a young earth timetable in spite of overwhelming scientific evidence that the earth is well over 4.5 billion years old. Sounds like 'Biblicist Babel' is still on the rise.

Biosophy

Biosophy means the wisdom (*vidya*) of life' and fosters the science and art of intelligent living based on the biological awareness and practice of spiritual values, ethical-social principles, and character qualities essential to personal freedom and social harmony. Biosophy was most likely introduced by Swiss humanist, Ignaz Paul Vitalis Troxler in the early 1800s. (I mention him because he was a free-thinker who challenged unquestioned answers—our kind of guy!)

Blanket Pardon

Issue yourself a blanket pardon. Forgive yourself for any mistakes you have made, and forgive anyone who may have injured or harmed you in any way.

Blingology

An over-abundance of, and attachment to, bling is the 'minus' touch of materiality. "To bling or not to bling?" isn't really the question. The real question is: How much bling do you need before you don't feel the need for more bling?

If a pickpocket finds himself at a world conference of spiritual shakers and movers who represent all of the major faith traditions, all he sees are their pockets.

Book of Life

I believe the 'Book of Life' the scriptures mention is your 'Quantum Self,' which is the quantum record of every thought, feeling, choice, and action you make—in each of your states of being—so that each nano-step of your spiritual unfoldment (the conscious return to your *True Spiritual Self*) is recorded. Nothing is lost because your essence is Pure Universal Consciousness particularized as you. (See Akashic Records reference.)

Boot Camp

Each human incarnation and reincarnation experience, each level of a spiritual initiation, every skin school life lesson we face, each attempt we make to raise our egocentric awareness to its higher spiritual nature are all boot camps.

The consequences of our decisions are boot camps. And oftentimes our poor decisions turn out to be 'kick-in-the-butt' camps.

Each meditation experience is a boot camp because you enter it as a new you with the live ammunition of each day's experiences coming at you at the speed of consciousness.

Both Human and Divine

Scholars debate whether Jesus was both human and divine or simply divine at birth. The opposing views are called *dyophysite* (the Christ as Jesus had two loosely united natures, one purely human and the other purely divine) and monophysitism (the Christ as Jesus had but a single nature, his human nature being absorbed into his divinity at birth). In my opinion, we like Yeshua (Jesus), have but a 'single nature, our human nature being absorbed into our divinity at birth'—but because we are unaware of our divine genealogy, we have two loosely united natures, one purely human and the other purely divine since we have not fully aligned our egocentric nature with our Divine Nature (Logos Nature).

Bronze Serpent

Although I'm going to mention the Israelite story of Moses' bronze snake, I'm not going to park there for very long. Why? It's a cute Old Testament religious story, but, MetaSpiritually speaking, there's soooo much more to serpent symbolism. For starters, according to the literal tradition, following their exodus from Egyptian captivity, the Israelites grew impatient and disrespectful of Moses' leadership and Yahweh's guidance. They complained and then rebelled. So, God (the anthropomorphic meme deity of the Old Testament) sent 'fiery serpents' to bite them! (God did that, of course, because He loved them!) For the sake of the ones who were repentant, Moses was instructed by the meme God to erect a 'serpent of bronze' on a pole to heal those who looked upon it (Numbers 21:4-9):

"Moses made a brazen snake (*nehushtan*) and placed it on a high pole. When anyone was bitten by a snake and looked at the bronze snake, they lived (*chaiah*)" (Numbers 21:9, *New International Version*).

MetaSpiritually, the bronze serpent mentioned in the *Book of Numbers* and in several of the subsequent references above is the serpentine kundalini energy and the pole is your spinal column. '*Nin Giz Zida*' is another name for the Hindu concept of kundalini which is a Sanskrit word that means 'coiled up' or 'coiling up like a snake.' In its purely Sanskrit etymology, kundalini refers to the mothering intelligence behind yogic awakening and spiritual deepening that leads to altered states of higher consciousness. Actually, the symbolism of snakes coiled around a staff is an ancient representation of kundalini physiology, when you think about it. The staff represents our spinal column and the snakes (ida and pingala) being twin energy channels.

Buddha-ful

When it comes to validating the reliability of the truth of a claim, whether it comes from a religious leader or scientist, Buddhism gives the greatest credibility and authority to experience first, then sound reason and discernment, and finally to scriptural integrity. The Buddha himself invited his followers not to accept the validity of his teachings just because he shared them or even simply because they revered him.

Bumped-Up Theology

I invite you to leave the embedded religious theology and scriptural literalism of your youth behind. I encourage you to have the willingness – and good sense – to loosen your hold on an anthropomorphic god meme in the sky who is separate from your True Essence and get a grip on a greater reality: you are a human expression of the Eternal Presence (Pure Universal Consciousness) expressing Itself as you. So, I embolden you to 'up your consciousness' to the realization that you are divine at your core. And by all means, leave the fractured orthodoxy of pediatric, literalist religion behind since it has your servitude in mind. So, unplug yourself from pediatric theology.

Burn Notice

Based on the USA Network TV series *Burn Notice*, burn notices are issued by intelligence agencies to discredit or announce the dismissal of agents who are considered to have become unreliable. However, I use burn notices as metaphors for error thoughts, words and actions that discredit our professed spiritual growth. Their habitual use suggests that humankind is still living in a hellish state of consciousness, which makes our professed commitments to spiritual growth both suspect and unreliable.

Burnt Offerings

MetaSpiritually speaking, burnt offerings have absolutely nothing to do with sacrificing animals as part of unconscionable ceremonial worship to an anthropomorphic god meme in the sky who expects that type of subservience. Burnt offerings represent our disciplined self-purification and self-cleansing. As we advance toward *Self-Realization,* the spiritual truths we learn and build into our daily lives 'burn' the dross of error from our consciousness and physical form. The 'fragrance' of expiated karma is transmuted (offered up, raised) to its ethereal spiritual essence which underwrites our True Spiritual Nature.

ॐ   ॐ   ॐ

Calling

If you want to experience terrifying, unsettling silence and raised eyebrows, tell the world you're going full-time as a writer or a dancer or a speaker or a Unity minister. Or mention that you're going to become a metaphysician or non-traditional healer. Looks of disbelief and concern for your welfare—not to mention your sanity—will register on the faces of those you have just shocked. They know, as well as you, that those who choose to write, speak, dance, paint, sculpt, heal, or represent a non-denominational spiritual ministry for a living have never had an easy time of it in all of recorded history. But do it you must in response to a deeply ingrained soul urge.

Cain and Abel

For centuries mainstream religion has missed the deeper spiritual meaning of this age old archetypical story by labeling it as the literal struggle between two brothers. However, the perennial struggle these archetypical brothers represent is *within each of us.* Cain and Abel, as well as all of the twins I mention below, represent two very different natures within us, and the grand struggle they symbolize involves the unnecessary incompatibility between these two natures, one which is Logos-centric and the other egocentric.

As a matter of fact, all over the world, mythologies record the dissension between a pair of brothers, oftentimes twin brothers, who are at odds. For example, in Hindu mythology, the Ashvins were a pair of handsome Vedic gods who were twins and who were mythologized to be divine physicians and protectors. One twin symbolized sunrise and the other sunset, making them opposites.

In Egyptian mythology Seth murders his twin brother Osiris (the Egyptian Christ) and puts the body of Osiris in a chest on the river. When the boat arrives at the opposite shore, from that place springs up an acacia tree, which grows up around the chest to protect Osiris. It's also believed that Roman centurions cut the crown of thorns they placed around the head of Jesus of Nazareth from an acacia tree. According to ancient traditions acacia wood symbolizes the power and significance of sacrifice.

There were Ašvieniai twins, in Lithuanian lore, who were very similar to twin gods in Latvian and Baltic mythologies. Both of these brothers are reported to be modeled after Roman and Greek sibling deities.

Romulus and Remus, of Roman mythology, were twin sons of the god Mars and one of the Vestal Virgins. When the boys grew to adulthood, they decided to found a city. According to one story, Romulus began to lay out the walls of Rome, but the walls were only one stone high. His brother Remus mocked him by jumping over the 'curb-sized' walls, saying, "See how easily anyone can get over your so-called walls!" And Romulus is said to have replied, "But see what awaits anyone who does," and runs Remus through with a sword. (Looks like Remus got the point!)

Another pair of mythological twins are the Dioscuri twins, Castor and Pollux, who were sons of Zeus. They were horsemen and seafarers and were the origin of the Zodiacal sign Gemini. Their mother was Leda, but Castor was the mortal son of Tyndareus (the mortal king of Sparta) and Pollux was the divine son of the god Zeus, who had seduced Leda in the guise of a swan. The brothers later joined the crew of Jason and the Argonauts.

The tales of twin brothers who are at odds isn't over yet. Many scholars point to the similarities between the Sumerian tale of Emesh and Enten and the biblical tale of Cain and Able. The Emesh and Enten tale is 'the closest parallel to the Biblical Cain and Abel story' for a good reason. The Emesh and Enten tale is found on clay tablets from the 3rd millennium BCE while the oldest source of the Hebrew Bible is thought to have been written during the 1st century BCE. So, the Sumerian myth predates the Biblical account.

In the Sumerian tale, the god Enlil couples with the Earth, which gives birth to twin boys named Emesh and Enten. Emesh symbolizes the freshness of summer and Enten represents the dormancy of winter. Each brother brings an offering to Enlil, but Enten becomes angry with Emesh and the two brothers argue.

At this juncture, however, the similarities end. In the Sumerian tale, the boys' father god Enlil intervenes and decides in favor of Enten. Emesh accepts Enlil's ruling and the brothers reconcile. However, in the Hebrew Genesis account, Cain murders his brother Abel.

Before I describe the Cain and Able story in Genesis, Chapter 4, there's another Bible story about a pair of twin brothers who get into conflict with each other. It's the story of Jacob (also called Israel 'he who wrestles with God') and Esau (the hairy one). According to the Biblical account, Jacob flees from his twin brother Esau, whom he had tricked out of receiving their father Isaac's blessing which was customarily bestowed on the first-born.

MetaSpiritually, in all of these stories, the brothers are two sides of us (left and right hemisphere, head and heart, egocentric and Logos-centric) and aspects, thoughts, inclinations and propensities within us. Internal division and conflicting thoughts and feelings apply to all of us – men, women and children. We all have within our human personality both Cain and Abel, Emesh and Enten, Castor and Pollux, Romulus and Remus, Jacob and Esau, Ašvieniai and Ashvins.

So, let's take a look at the Biblical account of Cain and Abel. Abel's name literally means 'breath or spirit (*pneuma*),' our Higher Spiritual Nature. Cain's name means 'the personality that's created in each skin school lifetime and produces 'fruit of the sensory experience,' rather than of our Cosmic Spiritual Nature (Abel). Cain symbolizes our lower, sense-prone nature which is embodied in our earthly self. The story begins in Genesis Chapter 4. The scripture states:

"And Adam knew Eve his wife, and she conceived, and bare Cain, and said, I have gotten a man from the Lord."

Adam symbolizes the archetypical movement in mind that epitomizes the reasoning, reductionist, objective, logical, deductive, methodical and judgmental nature of our make-up. Adamic energies underwrite our left hemispheric brain-ness and are very much tied to our thoughts when we incarnate into human form.

Eve represents the archetypical pattern in our heart-centered awareness that epitomizes the nurturing, highly intuitive, wisdom-centered, subjective, unconditional love-oriented, social and emotive nature of our make-up. Eve energies underwrite our right hemispheric brain-ness and are connected very psychically to our feelings when we incarnate into human form.

The archetypical mythical couple, Adam and Eve, show us that if the polarities between the head and the heart and left hemisphere and right hemisphere do not fully resonate, the products of their union (Cain and Abel, Romulus and Remus, etc.) will exhibit the disequilibrium and conflict that characterize the original disconnect. And that's what happens in the story.

The Cain and Abel qualities within us - Cain (our incarnated left-brained hemisphere which is ego-centric and attached to the physical dimension) and Abel (our right-brained hemisphere that is Logos-centric and devoted to our spiritual dimension) must be in alignment. What's interesting is that Abel is not the one who struggles in the story. In the original Hebrew Abel is written Habel, which means 'empty of worldly or material attachments.'

On the other hand, the struggle comes from our Cain-ness because the unenlightened ego is always in a constant struggle to kill off our higher, more spiritual nature. The materialistic ego wants total control, because to sacrifice its temporal rulership is to die to our worldly self and let our Higher Spiritual Nature live through, in and as us!

"And in the process of time it came to pass, that Cain brought the fruit of the ground as an offering unto the Lord. And Abel, he also brought of the firstlings of his flock and of the fat thereof. And the Lord has respect unto Abel and to his offering: But unto Cain and to his offering he had not respect" (Gen. 4:3-6).

Our Cain-ness identifies solely with the physical senses. This is why we hesitate to sacrifice our egocentric personality (*persona*) to anything that seems spiritual. Given this mentality, the best things we can offer to our God Nature are the products of our physical senses.

When we offer up those kinds of worldly attachments, our Higher Spiritual Nature (God Essence) is vibrating at too high of a spiritual octave (is displeased) for the lower vibrational sensory attachments to register in our super-consciousness (Pure Universal Consciousness).

Since worldly offerings are left-brain generated 'fallout' based on earthy desires, we tend to feed our own selfishness first and what is left over—if anything—is relegated for our own spiritual growth and development: "First I'm going to have this career; first I have to win the lottery; first I must have a house; first I've got to finish my doctorate; first I've … , then I'll concentrate on my spiritual growth (give my offering to my God Nature)." That's our Cain-ness talking!

When we look beneath the literal interpretation we discover that Cain's fruits, the fruits of a worldly ego, have no lasting or permanent qualities and cannot provide us the lasting happiness, inner peace and joy that come from a disciplined and devoted truth walk.

In Genesis 4:8 Cain (our sense-addicted ego) kills (stifles, represses, denies) Abel (our spiritual tendencies)! Shortly after the 'murder' of our tendencies toward our Higher Nature, which symbolically represents our unenlightened ego reasserting its dominance over our human personality, our innate Divinity remains vital, but dormant (curses), and continues to underwrite our physical being (tells Cain that he will be 'a fugitive and a vagabond in the earth).

A few verses later the author of Genesis tells us that Cain "went out from the presence of the Lord, and dwelt in the land of Nod…" (Genesis. 4:16). The Hebrew word for 'Nod' means to 'wander, drift or stray.' This is another clue that the Land of Nod symbolizes a special kind of conscious existence. MetaSpiritually, 'to wander' implies vacillating in and out of higher thought processes by going from ordinary awareness to super-conscious awareness and back again into an ordinary awareness. It could also suggest reincarnating again and again into the physical realm (skin school).

As you can see, allegorically, the twin brother's battle takes place within us. It's a well-known theme throughout antiquity. Although our Cosmic Logos Nature underwrites our human nature, it's our human beingness that must choose to access our Divine Nature. You can stay stuck in your Cain-ness and repress your innate divinity (your Abel-ness) and awaken to who you really are —a very powerful spiritual being having a human experience.

Capital Punishment

Destructive human habits like over-consumption of alcoholic (ethanol) beverages, stress, over-exposure to the sun, meth (methamphetamines) and other illegal drug usage, consuming aspartame (artificial sugar in diet sodas), excessive caffeine use, vaping (e-cigarette usage) and smoking, and chronic negative emotions such as anger, anxiety and hatred are all forms of capital punishment that cause soul death which causes cell death.

Cellular Consciousness

The cellular level of Pure Universal Beingness expresses Itself as nerve cells, bone cells, muscle cells, blood cells, adipose cells, pancreatic cells, etc. Each cell in your body is a localized 'island of consciousness.' Each of your trillions of cells is a sacred tabernacle of 'frozen' *Cosmic Logos*. And these sacred tabernacles are connected—consciously. There's no denominational sparing because their biology is their theology, so to speak. From cell to soul and soul to cell, your cellular body is a highly-charged sacred ground of Pure Being.

What's interesting is that the *organelle* (any of a number of organized or specialized structures within a living cell) that coordinates the adjustments and reactions of a cell to its internal and external environments represents the cytoplasmic equivalent of a 'cellular brain.' At some point in your cellular unfoldment your cells formed cellular identities and 'intuited' the concept of 'self' and 'non-self' as a result of the 'separate self drive' of your egocentric mindset.

The Cellular Consciousness of Pure Universal Beingness is the allness of Pure Universal Beingness (the One Reality) being particularized as a cell. Essentially, your cells are carbon-based 'computer chips' that regulate cell functions and gene expression. Cells have a tensegrity structure that guides their decision-making abilities and shifts their energy. It doesn't take much of a leap in awareness to realize your 'cellular family' is composed of highly conscious beings.

Cellular Theology

Each cell, every molecule, each of your atoms is a sacred tabernacle of Pure Consciousness. These sacred tabernacles are connected and they're highly intelligent beings. There is no Interfaith posturing. Their biology is their theology. When you realize the significance of this invisible connection you'll honor your human soul's relationship to your *Higher Spiritual Self*. When you acknowledge this connection, from soul to cell and from cell to soul, your body becomes the highly-charged sacred ground of your being. When you achieve this perfect synchrony you'll experience the inner peace, joy, health, and wholeness which are the truth of you. So, *cell-ebrate your cell power!*

Centered Periphery

The closer you get to *Self-Realization* (becoming consciously one with your *Higher Spiritual Self* which is the Cosmic Logos in human form as you), the clearer it becomes to you that the 'Still Point' at both Its center (your soul singularity) and Its omniscient periphery (your Divine Nature) are one.

Chakraology

The seven major chakras (ethereal centers or sheaths), representing the cosmic emanations or states of consciousness, symbolize the seven key realms of cosmic manifestation that we matriculate through when travel from our highest spiritual essence between incarnations and morph into physicality, our lowest form of Self-referent essence. These emanations are 'cosmic super-strings' of conscious existence which are connected to the different phases of our over-all awareness as we reclaim the conscious awareness of our Divine Nature (one of the human forms of the One Reality, Pure Universal Consciousness).

For example, the most transcendent emanation, the Crown Chakra (Shamballa) is the Realm of Infinite Potential, our super-conscious aspect. The Brow Chakra is the Realm of Cosmic Clarity, the All Knowing aspect of our evolving awareness. The Throat Chakra is the Realm of Calling Things Into Manifestation, the formative (wavicle) aspect of us. The Heart Chakra is the Realm of Om, the door between the manifest and unmanifest, existence and non-existence, the center and circumference of the universe. The Solar Plexus Chakra is the Realm of Causal Currents, the subtle and gross aspects of our beingness. The Sacral Chakra is the Realm of Astral Forces, the aspect of us that contains our Ethereal Double. The Base Chakra is the Realm of Gross Matter, the aspect of us that ensures our connection to the material universe.

Your 72 centimeter journey (the length of your spinal column) toward enlightenment is comprised of seven levels of spiritual unfoldment, or stages of initiation. Each of these levels is represented by a defining chakra (golden candlestick). As you open yourself up to higher esoteric learning you'll find that the chakras are real – and that it's possible for everyone to experience his or her tremendous spiritual power. These wheel-like vortices of super-charged energy rotate around the spinal column and are the super-physical highways to enlightenment. They're the cosmic conduits of the powerful spiritual energies within you. (See Straight Is the Gate and Narrow Is the Way reference.)

Changeology

All change isn't necessarily growth, just like all movement isn't necessarily forward and activity isn't necessarily accomplishment.

Child Birth

In orthodox Jewish society, to refer to a son as the son of a woman is to cast public doubt on the legitimacy of his birth. It is a charge that implies being base-born (illegitimate).

Was Yeshua (Jesus) born in Bethlehem? Most likely not! According to Mark's Gospel he was born in Nazareth. To sell Jesus' messianic value, his birthplace was moved to Bethlehem.

Matthew refers to Yeshua's birth as a virgin birth and bases the story on an Isaiah 7:14 reference) The problem is, the word 'virgin' is not in the Isaiah scripture. The word Isaiah used was '*almah*' which means 'woman.' Isaiah doesn't use the Hebrew word '*bethulah*' which would refer to a 'virgin.' Isaiah was referring to Ahaz's wife who gave birth to Hezekiah who was to succeed Ahaz, his father.

Chiropractic Prayer

Chiropractic prayer (affirmative prayer) uses specific declarative statements that deny the illusionary power of outer appearances and follows up those declarations with positive affirmations that correct the subluxations of error thinking.

Choices

Most people keep themselves so busy and have gotten themselves so far behind that the future is gone before they get there. Some people, on the other hand, dream of noteworthy accomplishments, but fail to turn their dreams into reality. Too many people lose opportunities because they've lost themselves. And too many people have lost themselves because they are beside themselves with doubt, fear or pride. It doesn't have to be that way. Opportunities are one choice away.

Do you know that some people change their choices as a result of their values, while others change their values as a result of their choices?

Has it occurred to you that most people aren't fast enough to keep up with their poor choices?

How much difference do you think there is between the will to change and the whim to change?

Believe it or not it takes less energy and less worry to make wise choices. That's the amazing thing about making prosperity-affirming choices—your life tends to be clutter-free, abundance-rich, and filled with unlimited prosperity. My beautiful wife, Cher, and I can honestly and joyfully report that the cumulative effects of prosperous choices are WONDERFUL. We're grateful every day and keep ourselves available as the *human continuations* of our Spiritual Nature. We take the words of the *Cosmic Logos* as Jesus very seriously when Jesus assured us 2, 000 years ago that we "can have life, and have it more abundantly" (John 10:10). (See our *Cosmic Logos* reference.)

The Christ

The word 'Christ' comes from *Christos*, a Greek word meaning 'the anointed one.' It's the equivalent of the word Messiah (Mashiach in Hebrew). So the 'Christ' or Messiah in Biblical literature, was seen as the 'anointed one of God' (God's Only Begotten). Just so you know, in Biblical times, to be anointed by someone (generally a priest or religious leader) literally, was to have sacred oil poured on your head, because the God meme 'out there' has chosen you for 'his' special work on earth. Priests and kings, and occasionally prophets, were anointed. Kings were even anointed during their coronations rather than receiving the typical jeweled crown. The Jewish people were—are—expecting a great king to arise out of Israel who will be God's CEO (God's Chief

Executive Offspring) over the whole earth and that 'anointed executive' will come from the House of David.

The 'anointed Christ' (messiah) of the Christian and Jewish scriptures isn't the same thing as the *Cosmic Logos!* The 'Christ' is a religious label that has been attached to Yeshua (Jesus) to support the claim that he's the long-awaited messiah to free the Jewish people from repeated bondage and the world from 'sin.' The thing is, the *Cosmic Logos* did incarnate as Yeshua (Jesus). It incarnates as each one of us at our birth! The confusion is in the 'messianic' and 'anointing' terminology of the Jewish and Christian faithful. They misused the universal cosmic concept of the *Logoic Self (Cosmic Logos)* by localizing It, contextualizing It, as the 'Christ' who was born as the man Jesu—and no one else—in order to sell the prodigious carpenter's son as the 'anointed savior of the world' for religious and political purposes.

The 'Only Begotten' emanation of the One Reality (Pure Universal Consciousness) is Its formative (quantum) aspect called the *Cosmic Logos* which 'calls' physicality into existence!

According to New Testament writers, Jesus was the long-awaited-for flesh and blood king. What's interesting is, according to John's Gospel, Jesus explained that his kingdom was *not* of this world (John 18:37). I believe the 'kingdom' Yeshua (Jesus) was talking about is our super-consciousness (the Field of Infinite Potential, the Timeless Divine Essence of the One Reality expressed as the *Cosmic Logos*, our *Higher Spiritual Self*).

The Christ idea (the anointed one, messiah) was emotional wishcraft for a savior by a people who had been subjugated for centuries by foreign powers. They pled for a flesh and blood 'messiah,' hand picked by an anthropomorphic 'god in the sky' to save them and deliver them from captivity! I totally empathize with them. Who wouldn't want to be delivered from bondage, from centuries of suffering, from the darkness of captivity! I believe that emotionally-charged desire has been adopted by humankind, in general. The focus on an external 'savior' has caused us to look 'out there' for answers—and redemption—instead of inside of ourselves. Unfortunately, the vast majority of humankind has bought into a Self-negating script! There's no 'anointed one' or flesh and blood messiah! Why? Because we don't need one! We've never needed one! We're all born Divine. All of us are spiritual beings having a human experience. The 'Presence of God' is in our human DNA. It's the *Cosmic Logos* attribute (the Word) of the One Reality called God. It's the 'outer form' (the Ethereal Embodiment) of a Mindlike Beingness called Pure Universal Consciousness (my term for the One Reality, God, Ground of All Being and Non-Being, the Infinite Isness, the Absolute). Each of us is born with a *Higher Spiritual Self* which is the *Cosmic Logos* embodied as us! All we have to do is express our Divine Nature. There's no need to wait for anyone or anything – but ourselves – to get us out of our self-imposed captivity.

Angelus Silesius, the German mystic, expressed Meister Eckhart's perspective when he said, "Though Christ in Bethlehem a thousand times be born, and not within thyself, thy soul will be forlorn." This perspective is absolutely essential for understanding our Divine Nature because each of us is the human expression of the *Cosmic Logos* (what Eckhart and others call the Christ which is the Greek word for 'messiah' the 'anointed one') outpicturing Itself at the point of us in whatever dimension of being we find ourselves.

Christianity

If you believe in the traditional messianic (Christos) message, Christianity isn't necessarily about being a Christian, it's about being the best Christ you can be. As a matter of fact, if you modify the spelling of 'Christian' by dropping the 'n' and replacing it with an 'm' you get 'Christ I am.' Christianity, like the other world religions is exclusive in its beliefs. So, I prefer the affirmation 'Be the best *Self- Realized* spiritual being you can be.'

Christianity has many parking places. They're called denominations.

Churchianity

It's important for your spiritual growth to choose to move beyond memorizing and repeating literal interpretations of scripture. Otherwise, you may become a dogmatic, *religious victrola,* moving your lips without having been moved in your heart. Just like a CD or cassette plays recordings of sacred writings without understanding their meaning, many people who settle for superficial, literalist religiosity are unaware of the scriptural passage's deeper truths.

Religiously speaking, 'sin tax' is the penalty mainstream religion says we owe based on its faulty use of syntax when it comes to basing their religious beliefs on literal-only interpretations of sacred scripture.

Confidential Health Advisors

Confidential health advisors are the pacemakers, glucose monitors, an actual illness or dis-ease, concierge doctors, fevers, feelings of 'something not rightness' we get when we listen to our bodies, temperature thermometers, etc.

Consciousness

What we call the small 's' self is the ego's rendition of our human self which is the product, quantumly speaking, of a tangled hierarchy. The unenlightened ego's awareness is the small "s" self-awareness. However, our consciousness is a particularized consciousness of the One Presence Cher and I call Pure Universal Consciousness (God, Brahman, the Universal Self, the Infinite Isness, the Absolute) and as such is beyond the subject-object split. Our egoic self-awareness is the localized version of our nonlocal, unitive cosmic consciousness which is connected to the 'Field.'

Consciousness isn't an epiphenomenal effect of biology. Biology simply records the effects of the Pure Universal Consciousness in the material world manifold.

A turtle's shell grows at the same rate as the rest of the turtle, so there is hardly a need of concern of the turtle getting too fat for its shell. When the shell begins to look as if it is coming apart, it is merely growing; discarding portions of the old with incoming segments of new. As we grow, we too need to discard the things that are no longer working for us at our new spiritual level of awareness! So, I invite you to perform regular mental check-ups to be sure your thoughts, beliefs, values and attitudes are congruent with the Truth Principles you practice! Anything out of alignment needs to go!

Our consciousness is not lost after each incarnational/ reincarnational experience in spite of the dissolution of our physical envelop, because our physicality is a product of our consciousness. One of the tasks of our Quantum Self is to learn to master our physical envelops. (See Quantum Self reference in *More Straight Talk About Spiritual Stuff* book.)

Until the beginning of the 21st century no serious scientific research on the study of consciousness was attempted. Isn't that amazing! After centuries of neglect, the study of consciousness is being embraced by the neurosciences, quantum physics, epigenetics, biology, psychoneuroimmunology, and biocentrism. It's this shift in awareness that will bring us closer to dismantling both the dogma in fear-based religion and the dogma in heady science.

Conscious Satsang

Satsang is a Sanskrit word that means 'gathering together for the truth.' *Conscious satsang* refers to filling your consciousness with thoughts, intentions and inclinations of higher spiritual truths to show your devotion to your spiritual growth.

Cosmic Consciousness

The ancient doctrine of *panpsychism* comes close to the universal dimensions of the cosmic expression of Pure Universal Consciousness. This level of Cosmic Consciousness expresses Itself as universal and inter-dimensional aggregates that combine to produce specific conscious experience. It expresses a highly integrated and information-rich system of intra-differentiated states which foster a large repertoire of highly inter-differentiated states (parallel dimensions) that are universally connected.

Cosmic Logos

The Word, *Logos* (Greek), and *dabhar* (Aramaic) do not mean 'word' as understood linguistically. Instead, it means transcendental sound vibration, energy in motion, cosmic light, the subtle creative pulse of physicality, the throb of materialization. Those extended meanings bring a whole new paradigmic dimension to the age old definitions of 'the Word,' don't they!

The *Cosmic Logos* is the underlying non-empirical principle, pattern, matrix that expresses Itself as the quantum nature of the Universal Presence we call Pure Universal Consciousness by many names. It's the Limitless Light (*Ain Soph Aur*).

Cosmic Logos isn't an 'anointed' entity or a 'messianic' envoy sent to save humankind or any other 'kind' of being. It's the Pure Universal Consciousness expressing Itself as physicality. It's the world of subatomic and atomic particles, the world of forms, which are all quantum actualizations of the One Reality called Pure Universal Consciousness. There's no 'anointing' – or need for it - because that would imply that *something* 'anointed' *something else!* And that would imply separation when there is only a Universal Cosmic Singularity!

As the formative aspect of Pure Universal Consciousness, the *Cosmic Logos* (Word, *Spanda*) is the arbiter of eternal newness and expansion, catalytic beginningness, spontaneous freshness, invigorating finiteness and infiniteness, perennial birthing, and dynamic renaissancing.

Once the *Cosmic Logos* expresses Itself in all of Its materializations, it calls forth endless polarities: limitlessness and limits, boundarylessness and boundriedness, infiniteness and finiteness, beginningness and endness, materialness and immaterialness, abyssness and summitness, form and formlessness, locality and nonlocality, somethingness and nothingness, externality and internality, ever-present confinement and unlimited freedom.

In all mainstream religious systems the idea of an intermediate divine being between God and the world appears: the *Oum* of the Indians, the *Hom* of the Persians, the *Logos* of the Greeks, the *Memra* of the Jews, the *Christ* of Christianity. However, MetaSpiritually speaking, there's no intermediary! The manifest and unmanifest are simply qualities or aspects or continuations or expressions of the One Universal Reality.

In the *Gospel of John* (1:1-5) the literal interpretation says:

In the beginning was the Word, and the Word was with God, and the Word was God. The same was in the beginning with God. All things were made by him; and without him was not any thing made that was made. In him was life; and the life was the light of men. And the light shineth in darkness; and the darkness comprehended it not.

In order to elaborate on what I believe the Gospel writer meant, I'm going to offer the following MetaSpiritual interpretation of the *Logos Nature* he talked about in the first five verses:

The manifestation of this Universe was created by the Cosmic Logos, and the Cosmic Logos is the Absolute (Pure Universal Consciousness) expressing Itself as physicality. All things in this Universe and all of the other universes have been emanated and evolved from the Cosmic Logos; and nothing has existed here or anywhere else except through the dynamic formulative aspect of the Cosmic Logos. The Cosmic Logos is Divine Life Itself; and that Life underwrites the spiritual light in humankind and the light in all things. The light (energetics) of the Cosmic Logos shines forth from the unmanifest of the Pure Universal Consciousness as the vibrational throb of manifestation.

So, the *Cosmic Logos* is the All-Ensouling Consciousness and Life of Manifestation in all of its planetary and human forms. Essentially, It's the *Living Universe* itself.

The incarnate 'Word of God' is Its physical (quantum) aspect. One of It's unlimited essences is as the manifested Absolute in the world of form. Its high level of knowing and beingness is called Pure Universal Consciousness which is available to all of us since we are the *Cosmic Logos* expressing Itself in physical form as us! The symbolic imagery of God speaking in mainstream religious literature illustrates the metaphysical truth that the Word, or *Cosmic Logos,* is the potentializing aspect of God (the One Reality). It's the One Reality's cosmic beingness which underwrites all manifestation. It's the Eternal Isness which forms Itself into light, sound, vibration, and energy. (See the *Word* reference in this book; the *Arche, Spanda* [the *Cosmic Logos,* the *Word*], and *Apeiron* references in our *More Straight Talk About Spiritual Stuff* book; and Word of God reference in *Straight Talk About Spiritual Stuff* book.)

The *Cosmic Logos* figure described in the *Book of Revelation* could represent a composite of the seven sacred planets: It has the snowy-white hair of Kronos (Father Time), the blazing eyes of wide-seeing Zeus, the sword of Arcs, the shining face of Helios, and the *chiton* and girdle of Aphrodite; his feet are of mercury, the metal sacred to Hermes, and his voice is like the murmur of the ocean's waves (many waters), alluding to Selene, the Moon-Goddess of the four seasons and of the waters].

All manifestation is, in a sense, frozen *Logos*. It's the *logosophy* (the neuroplasticity of spiritual revelation). The *Cosmic Logos* takes many forms (which in and of themselves are composed of trillions of forms) that can manifest as: a Planetary *Logos*, Solar *Logos*, Galactic *Logos*, Inter-Galactic *Logos*, Universal *Logos*, Multiverse *Logos*, Megaverse *Logos*, etc.

In Apocryphal writings, the 'Word' is described as a Being of Light, proceeding essentially from the Ultimate Reality. It's a Cosmic Image, a Co-occupant of the divine throne. It's a real and independent principle, revealing the Godhead in the world and mediating between the world and God. (I substitute the 'Beingness of Pure Universal Consciousness' for 'being of light' because consciousness is a gazillion times faster than the speed of light. I also take any mention of 'co-occupancy' out, since I believe there's only the One Universal Reality with Its myriad of attributes. Forgive me, but I also discard any mention of separation between the manifest and unmanifest since both are simply different attributes of the One Universal Reality).

The *Cosmic Logos,* in all of Its manifested forms, is the Finiteness of the Infinite.

The *Cosmic Logos* is the center and circumference of the universe as well as the Transcendent Universal Beingness beyond any and all of the universes, because the *Cosmic Logos* extends beyond the Multiverse which spawns universes. We're the 'spiritual creators' of the particular universe we're inhabiting as we seek to understand our *True Self* and Its relationship to the transcendentalness of the *Cosmic Logos.*

You mock your *Cosmic Logos Nature* when you doubt yourself, belittle yourself, and fear the difficulties the world of outer appearances tosses your way.

The *Cosmic Logos* doctrine is believed to have originated with Heraclitus of Ephesus (550-480 BCE) who was associated with the mystery school at the Artemis Temple (Artemision Temple) in Ephesus. He has been referred to as the 'weeping philosopher' for lamenting the "needless unconsciousness of humankind," and as the 'obscure' for his misunderstood esoteric writings. He was a brilliant pre-Socratic philosopher who saw our relationship with the Divine as one of indivisible oneness, especially our *Logos Nature.* I mention him in this book because I strive to be just as 'unplugged' when it comes to discovering our *True Logos Nature* as Heraclius was five hundred years before Yeshua (Jesus) was born.

One more thing about the *Cosmic Logos* concept. Besides Heraclitus of Ephesus, there were others in antiquity who discovered our *Logos Nature* and taught it before the cosmic vision 'disappeared' from Christian and the world's consciousness. I'm mentioning a few of them; however, there probably were only a few of them who thought that far outside the proverbial religious box. Here they are: Anaximander of Miletus (610-546 BCE); The Stoics embraced the Logos idea, influenced by Zeno of Cleanthes (350-264 BCE); Poseidonius (135-51 BCE); Philo of Alexandria (25 BCE-50 CE); Marcus Aurelius (121-180 CE); Clement of Alexandria (150-215 CE); Hippolytus of Rome (170-235 CE); Origen of Alexandria (185-254 CE). The *Cosmic Logos* mantle is once again lifted from the 'darkness' by the following notables:

Cyril of Alexandria (376-444 CE); Maximus the Confessor (580-662 CE); John of Damascus (675-749 CE); Hildegard von Bingen (1098-1179 CE); (Nicholas of Cusa (1401-1464 CE); Catherine of Genoa (1447-1510 CE); Helena Petrovna Blavatsky (1831-1891); Annie Besant (1847-1933); Charles Webster Leadbeater (1854-1934); Rudolf Steiner (1861-1925 CE); Alice Bailey (1880-1949); Pierre Teilhard de Chardin (1881-1955 CE); Geoffrey Hodson (1886-1983); Hans-Werner Schroeder (1931- CE); Matthew Fox (1940- CE). I, too, share this august group's *Cosmic Logos* perspective; however, I wouldn't classify myself as a notable.

The logos *spermtikos* (the seedlike *Logos* that underwrites us) was a well-known concept in Stoicism, but was considered as a separate logoic emanation from the *Logos* of the cosmos. From that line of thought the concepts of the *Planetary Logos* and *Solar Logos* of the Theosophists were born. Unfortunately, the cosmic dimension of the logos was buried (localized) in the man called Yeshua (Jesus) by Christian religious fundamentalists, losing its global and cosmic incarnation status. My idea of the *Cosmic Logos* is that It incarnates as EACH OF US in human form at the time of our birth in skin school (and in each of our 'births' in other dimensions of being). You've already been introduced to my 'inconvenient truth' perspective in the comments I've made up to now and throughout this book.

Cosmic Urge

The desire for each of us to explore as many different dimensions of being as we can to experience the totality of quantumness is what we call the cosmic urge. It's this perennial urge that drives us toward *Self Realization* and globalized thinking, being and doing.

Creation Myths

The Jewish and Christian creation stories were probably based on the older seven day Babylonian creation myth called the *Enûma Eliš* (as early as the 18th-16th centuries BCE, or perhaps as late as the 8th -7th centuries BCE). This ancient text saw the universe as formless and empty with the only existing thing prior to creation as a gigantic primordial water abyss. It's described as a 'watery chaos' from which everything else appeared. Many scholars, as well as my curious self, believe the Book of Genesis, where the spirit of God is reported as moving upon the dark face of the waters, is borrowed from Hindu and Babylonian creation myths. I'll say a little bit (more than a tweets worth) about the Hindu creation myth next.

In Hindu and Vedic cosmologies, there was nothing in the beginning of the Universe but darkness. The Supreme Unmanifested being created the primordial waters and established his seed into it. According to Vedic cosmology, this celestial embodiment (creator deity's emanation) turned into a golden womb (golden egg) from which everything else appeared. The Upanishads call it the Soul of Brahman, and say that the 'egg' floated around in emptiness and the darkness of non-existence before it produced manifestation. (See the compelling Arche reference in our book entitled *More Straight Talk About Spiritual Stuff.*)

Here's a snapshot of other creation myths I think you'll find interesting: The *Kumulipo* creation myth is a Hawaiian story that posits the world was created over a cosmic night (actually a series of nights). The *Cheonjiwang* Bonpuri is a Korean creation myth where *Cheonjiwand* (King of the Heavens and Earth) has his sons separate the sky and earth so there can be life. According to Chinese mythology, *Pangu* (the creator god) formed the universe out of the formless chaos. He separated Yin from Yang with a swing of his giant axe, and created the Earth and the Sky. In the Sumerian creation myth the gods (An, Enlil, Enki and Ninhursanga) created the conditions for life.

A Siberian myth, called the *Tungusic* creation myth, held that nothing existed but a vast primordial ocean. Then Buga (the chief Siberian deity) set fire to the ocean, and the flames consumed much of the water, exposing dry land. Next Buga created the light and separated it from darkness. Then he made two beings, a man and a woman.

According to Zulu mythology, *Unkulunkulu* (the Supreme Creator) created everything, from land and water to man and the animals. In the Finnish creation epic, *Kalevala*, the creator god, *Väinämöinen*, created the universe from chaos and from a cosmic egg. The egg whites turned into the moon and stars, and the yolk became the sun. In the creation myth of the Kuba of Central Africa, the creator god, *Mbombo* created the sun, moon and stars by vomiting them up. He then created men and animals the same way. (So, the universe—and us—seem to have been regurgitated). These are only a few of the hundreds of creation myths, of course, but much of their content is similar with much more showing the diversity—and bizarreness—of humankind's search for its divine genealogy.

Crown of Thorns

According to three of the canonical Gospels, a woven crown of thorns was placed on the head of the *Cosmic Logos* as Jesus during his crucifixion. However, that's not the 'crown of thorns' I'm going to describe. MetaSpiritually, the 'crown of thorns' symbolizes the highly vivified and spiritualized twelve pair of cranial nerves that surround the interior of our head like a crown. When we become fully illumined they transform our perfected nervous system into a glorified body of light. This 'crown' signals our having gained conscious immortality (a halo of light). The 12 pair of cranial nerves are: olfactory, optic, motor oculi, trochlear, trifacial, abducent, facial, auditory, glosso pharyngeal, pnumogastric, spinal accessor, and hypoglossal. (See the Crown of Thorns MetaSpiritually Interpreted article on our website: TheGlobalCenterForSpiritualAwakening.com for a more detailed explanation.)

the Crucifixion of Jesus

I believe an incredibly mystical and psychically-talented spiritual adept named Yeshua of Nazareth (Jesus) was crucified on a cross just outside of Jerusalem over 2, 000 years ago. However, I'm also convinced that the stories surrounding his ministry and crucifixion were remastered Jewish midrash (liturgy) to sell him as the long awaited Jewish messiah. I also believe he attained full

Self-Realization (completely aligned his human self with his *Higher Spiritual Nature*). He had been here (in skin school on the earth plane) many times and had reincarnated again to help lead us toward Self-Realization. He was an incredibly enlightened and spiritually illumined being who had achieved conscious oneness with his true identity: the One Reality (Pure Universal Consciousness) expressing Itself as him in human form!

MetaSpiritually speaking, crucifixion means 'crossing out all of our individual human error and karmic baggage' by totally and completely subordinating our egocentric nature to our highly super-conscious Divine Nature. Being crucified (transforming our physical body into its New Jerusalem embodiment from an esoteric Christianity perspective) is a Crown Chakra moment. (See the Etherealization and New Jerusalem references in this book and our book entitled *The Book of Revelation: New Metaphysical Version*.)

ॐ ॐ ॐ

Dancing

Cher and I began ballroom dancing as a spiritual practice in 1998 and discovered a new level of partnership and "soulmateness" that has enriched both our personal and professional lives. We competed nationally as an amateur couple in the American Smooth and Rhythm DanceSport Championships. Although we don't compete anymore we perform choreographed routines for showcases and exhibitions, "invent" our own trademark routines, and dance socially for non-competitive fun. And like Friedrich Nietzsche's sentiments said so many years ago: "Everyday (we) count wasted in which there has been no dancing." For us, dancing is a moving mindfulness meditation. Each element is a mindful step; every pattern is a spiritual path; every dance, in its totality, is a cosmic union with the energies of our combined divine natures.

Darkness

The Masonic formula, *T'ien Ti Huei,* asserts that the task of the masters is to "destroy the darkness, and restore the light." Darkness represents the unawareness of, or outright rejection of, our innate divinity. Choosing darkness over light (our path to Self-Realization) keeps us sense-soaked and unaware of our divine status—to our own detriment. Restoring the light is our privilege —and responsibility—as a spiritual being having a human experience.

Dasein Dilemma

Dasein is a German word that means 'being immersed in the primal nature of being in whatever dimension of being you inhabit.' It has also been described as meaning 'presence or existence.' It refers to the experience of being that is peculiar to us, as self-referent conscious beings. So, it's a form of beingness that's aware of and must confront such issues as personhood, mortality, and the dilemma or paradox of living in relationship with other human beings while being ultimately alone with oneself. I have extended the metaphor to describe our choice, as spiritual beings who chose to incarnate into physicality (worldliness) to fully understand the limits of our cosmic personhood. This concept is similar to Okakura Kakuzo's concept of *das-in-der-Welt-sein* (being-in-the-worldness, worldhood or worldliness). It also reminds me of being in the world, but not of the world – which has always been true for all of us spiritual beings who have left the etherealness of Spirit for the temptations of matter.

Death (Graduation, Transition, Retirement)

Each 'death' experience is a lifting of the veil of illusion. Whether we reincarnate into a human form again or incarnate into a new dimension of higher beingness, our life task will be to become consciously aware of who we really are – the One Presence expressing Itself as us.

For the attuned MetaSpiritualist,
death is not a grave matter.

When we graduate (make our transition) from our current skin school experience, our physical form recycles (metamorphosizes, dies), but our eternal beingness goes on to experience another state of being.

Here's why it's important to be in a meditative and prayerful state of mind when you are close to your earthly graduation (death, transition). The front half of your physical body (metaphorically, the West – which houses the lungs and five physical senses) is tied to the sense perceptions of your egocentric nature. The back half of your physical body (the East – with the spinal column and chakras) is tied to your inner Divine Nature. The lower part of your body (the South) is tied to the three lower chakras which are still influenced by external sensory perceptions. And the upper part of your body (the North) is tied to the four higher chakras of the Sacred Path which allows you spiritual clarity and an illumined consciousness. All of the above descriptions are a preamble to this observation: The most favorable state of mind to be in at your skin school graduation is a higher state of consciousness (North) where both your Brow and Crown Chakras are open. Leaving your physical garment (body) as you experience the inner peace, tranquility and transcendence associated with these highest chakra energies will keep you awakened to higher vibratory thoughts that will help guarantee your liberation from future reincarnations into the particular dimension you are exiting – if that's your desire. Your 'awakened exit' will definitely contribute to your Self-Realization which will remain available to you as an awakened spiritual being.

Dehypnotization

You have the wherewithal to move beyond the self-imposed hypnotic trance sprung on you by a crafty, but unenlightened ego. Your puppetlike obedience to a warped ego will keep you in the proverbial cloud of unknowing. Your dehypnotization begins when you realize the truth of who you are: the One Reality expressing Itself in human form as you! Once you blink yourself out of your self-imposed trance, you can become *Self Realized, Self Fulfilled,* and *Self Complete.*

Déjà Vu All Over Again

We meet ourselves hundreds, even thousands of times in the reincarnational disguises we create on our way to our *Self-Realization*. If the truth be told, reincarnation isn't a necessary condition for enlightenment. Enlightenment doesn't have to be a long journey. When we consciously connect with our I Am Nature (the One Reality that's the Ground of All Being and Non-Being) we become enlightened—and we can morph into our enlightenment in one lifetime if we conscientiously and unapologetically seek our *Self Definition*. In my opinion, the perfect déjà vu experience is *déjà vuing* with my Higher Spiritual Nature which is the 'True Me' before I became the 'Earthbound Me.'

Denominational Criticism

Instead of hurtfully picking holes in each other's religious beliefs, let's pick the 'Whole' in all of us by focusing on our oneness and spiritual genealogy.

Depression

One reason depression is such a global pandemic is that we have forgotten to include True North (*Higher Spiritual Nature*) on our collective mental map of who we are and what we've come here to do.

Directionally Challenged

MetaSpiritually speaking, being directionally challenged means trying to please a fictional god meme 'out there' separate from you who either rewards you or punishes you; pursuing a purely egocentric path of worldly fantasies and addictions that diminish you and imprison you; opting for base instincts instead of spiritual aspirations; and choosing a life of self-aggrandizement instead of a life devoted to Self-Realization and service to others.

Divine Abidings

The Buddha taught four kinds of contemplation designed to develop a sound symbiotic relationship with other living beings. The four are: *metta*, which means 'loving-kindness,' *karuna*, which equates with 'compassion,' *mudita* which means 'gladness for others' success,' and *upekkha*, which means 'onlooking equanimity.' These four are called Divine Abidings (*brahma-vihara*), probably because when we express any of them for even a moment we live for that moment in our elevated spiritual essence. In the Buddha's teaching these four Divine Abidings are the greatest of all worldly virtues. They are certainly 'abidings' that, if incorporated into your spiritual practice, would give you immense traction on your way to your own enlightenment.

Divine Genealogy

Knowing your divine genealogy allows you to walk through the smoke screens of doubt, fear, ridicule, betrayal, and the illusion of the separation between your human nature and your Divine Nature.

Divinely Ordering

I invite you to be very careful when you refer to Divine Order as something 'out there,' something external that is rigid and imposed upon you by some anthropomorphic celestial deity. It's my firm belief that Divine Order should be changed from a noun to an adverb/verb combination: Divinely Ordering! It's an internal cosmic ability available to you. Contrary to what you've been taught, and Cher and I were taught by well-meaning religious teachers, I don't believe Divine Order is some external cosmic force that acts upon us. I believe divinely ordering our good is the creative process of Mind–Idea–Expression. It's an intentional act of creation on our part. We can divinely order good or we can misapply our intentionality and create egocentric error expressions. A Divine Idea can be expressed spiritually or selfishly. Spiritually expressed it's a capital "D" Divine Idea. Selfishly expressed it is 'diddlysquat idea' since a Divine Idea has been misapplied.

The reason all things can work together for good is because you can work all things together for good. It's you, as an extension of the power of your *Higher Spiritual Self,* that can divinely order all of your earthly experiences and turn millstones into milestones when you turn *diddlysquat order* into Divine Order. Divinely ordering your good is accomplished when you divinely order your experience from the consciousness of your oneness with the One Reality (Infinite Isness, God, Pure Universal Consciousness). *Diddlysquat order* is a millstone perspective. It means allowing your fractured and frightened ego to tempt you into believing that you are separated from your Divine Nature, that you aren't a divine being, and that all good things must come to an end. Good things never end! They underwrite everything in the form of possibilities and probabilities.

What you need to remember most is that you are always divinely ordering your human experience. There's always an order to what you're doing! You may not always use it at your highest, most elevated level of consciousness. Sometimes you are divinely ordering your life, and other times you are manifesting what Cher and I love to call "diddlysquat order!"

If you believe you're *"exactly where you're supposed to be"* or *"should be"* because some divine puppeteer 'up there' is pulling your strings, I invite you to *"stop shoulding on yourself."* If you're where you are supposed to be, or should be, or ought to be, or had better be, it's because you're there by right of your own consciousness—not somebody else's or something else's.

If it's all in 'Divine Order' it's because you have divinely ordered it.

How often have you heard people use this phrase as a statement of resignation: *"It's all in Divine Order"*—meaning it's out of my hands, out of my control. It's already pre-determined by the Divine Order default police who know what's best for me. MetaSpiritually speaking, Divine Order isn't an external God-generated fiat or something a celestial deity imposes upon you. Divine Order isn't an event. It's a process. It's not a noun. It's a verb. It's not a pre-determined outcome. It's a pre-emptive course of action on your part, as a spiritual being in human form, to manifest something visible from the invisible.

Success, happiness, and prosperity work the same way because they are divinely ordered! Unfortunately, many people upset the timing by holding onto their fears, doubts, assumptions, greed, material attachments, unforgiveness, and illusions of a God meme 'out there' who dispenses favors to some and withholds good from others. Have the courage—and good sense—to divinely order your good and contribute to the good of others!

Dogs Smell Cancer and Diabetes

Studies have confirmed the ability of trained dogs (Labrador retrievers, Australian shepherds, German shepherds, poodles, dachshunds, Dobermans, collies and Portuguese water dogs) to detect skin cancer melanomas by just sniffing the skin lesions. Studies of dogs and cancer detection are based on the fact that cancerous cells release different metabolic waste products than healthy cells in the human body. The difference of smell is so significant that dogs are able to detect it even in the early stages of cancer.

Also, some researchers have proven that dogs can detect prostate cancer by simply smelling patients' urine. Others can gauge the blood sugar levels in diabetics, warn allergic owners away from peanuts, or detect when people with narcolepsy are about to fall asleep. People with phenylketonuria (or PKU) tend to smell musty. A faulty or missing digestive enzyme makes people with trimethylaminuria (or TMAU) smell fishy. Untreated diabetics can smell like nail-polish remover. The reason I'm including this research in my spiritual briefs is to remind us that our interconnectedness with all living things can be fantastically medicinal and holistic if we embrace our inherent oneness. (See Spider Silk Surgery.)

Dogma

The spiritual view of dogma is contrary to a religious perspective. For example, dogma spelled backwards can be formed into two words 'am god.' This reversal is much more than a simple semi-palindrome or reversgram—which are terms that refer to words spelled backwards. However, the significance of 'am god' as the reversgram of 'dogma' uncovers a universal spiritual truth that defines the extraordinary difference between spirituality and religion. Religious dogma is characterized by fanatical close-mindedness and unquestioned adherence to specific beliefs, despite compelling evidence to the contrary. Spirituality holds that, in terms of our present knowledge and understanding, we're all indivisible continuations of the One Reality (God) expressing Itself in human form as us. Wasn't it the *Cosmic Logos* as Jesus who said, "Ye are gods?"

Dogma isn't only a hardening of the attitude, but a hardening of your BS (belief system).

Warning: Open-mindedness may be hazardous to your dogmatic mindset.

Dogma isn't a guidepost, it's a hitching post that'll keep you tied to a narrow, high-walled religious belief system that leaves little, if any, opportunity for religious growth, let alone spiritual growth.

Every minute you're buried in dogma, you lose sixty seconds of enlightenment.

Hanging white-knuckled onto religious dogma keeps your hands in fists, your amygdala in gear, and your mind closed.

As young metaphysicians, Cher and I had gotten out of the dogmatic religious box years ago. This isn't arrogance or harsh judgmentalness. It's simply an unquenchable appetite for expanding our MetaSpiritual perspective in our search for spiritual Truths.

Never get into the deep end of superficial dogma. It's anti-intellectual and anti-intuitive, and anti-commonsensical. It's mindless mindlessness, wacky wackiness. It's being stuck in myopic stuckishness.

As long as the embers of an anthropomorphic God meme in the sky are fanned by dogma, the relevance of mainstream Christianity will continue to erode.

One of the not-so-noticeable drawbacks of entrenched religious dogma is that the faithful suffer from the mere excess of mindless obedience to unquestioned answers.

Dogma is a 'walled in' religious mindset gone berserk. It's the banishment of an open mind that embraces esoteric perspectives, sound science, and common sense.

The epitome of irrationality is thinking irrational dogma is rational.

Dogma asphyxiates itself on its own lack of depth. It's a 'fenced in' religious perspective that's filled with smidgeons of false assumptions, pinches of inaccuracies, and light touches of misconceptions concerning the nature of things. It's fear-based religious indoctrination.

More and more people are realizing that organized religion's fixation on perpetuating its dogmatic glaucoma, patriarchal governance, repression of women, same sex bigotry, external God meme focus, and literal-only interpretations of sacred scripture will not provide the spiritual guardrails or the smooth escalator ride needed for them to pursue their own spiritual path.

Questioning dogmatic religious views turns out to be commonsensical, and much more fulfilling, than blind obedience and mindless compliance to fossilized beliefs.

None of us born a dogmatist. It takes learned helplessness and fear, developing an irresponsible sense of institutionalized control, a high regard for mindless propaganda, and close-mindedness to become a card-carrying dogmatist.

Double Jeopardy

Some debilitating forms of double jeopardy are self-limiting beliefs that become a way of life; an error thought that morphs into an errant choice; an ill-conceived choice that becomes a disastrous action; allowing one self-negating addiction to spawn another; and so on.

Dualism

Besides getting rid of the illusory division between space and time, wave and particle, energy and matter, spiritual and cosmic, quantum physicists are doing away with the basic dualism of subject versus object, thus transcending our understanding of dualism and showing that when we combine spirituality and science, we'll create a richer and more meaningful spiritual path to enlightenment.

Dweller in the City

The Dweller in the City (*Purusha*) is your *Logos Nature* embodied as your earthly body. It's derived from the Sanskrit '*pura*' which means city or body, and '*usha*' a derivative of the verb '*vas*,' to dwell. However, in a very real sense, your *Logos Nature (Divine Nature)* doesn't 'dwell' in you – It is you in human form. Your human body is a rented vehicle that allows you to motor around the planet.

Dweller on the Threshold

The Dweller on the Threshold is the unredeemed (unenlightened) aspect of your human personality (dimensional personality) that's built up over many lifetimes. It takes the form of the sum total of forces of your lower physical nature (quantum self) as expressed in the personality (*vyaktitva*) prior to *Self-Realization*. The 'dweller' or 'guardian' could very well be a collection (quorum) our negative karma that hasn't been expiated between incarnations. And the 'threshold' could describe the cusp or doorway that leads from our egocentric consciousness to our *Logos Consciousness*. (See the

Quantum Self reference and the other references to *Quantum Self* throughout this book; see *Logos* references.)

ॐ   ॐ   ॐ

Earth

You're not separate from the Earth. You may have a consciousness of being separate from nature and its inhabitants (animals, plants, insects, etc.). However, the carbon in your breath comes from the vegetables you eat, the nitrogen atoms in your muscles comes from the blue sky, the phosphorus in your bones is loaned to you from the waves of a ancient ocean, the calcium in your teeth was mined from rocks by mushrooms, your teeth and bones are composed of calcium phosphates that come from the Earth's surface, the hydrogen and oxygen atoms in your sweat came from the tail of a comet, the iron in your blood once came from an exploding star. You are composed of hydrogen atoms and subatomic particles like quarks, leptons, and gluons that were present at the 'big bang' that created our universe. The nitrogen in your DNA came from the interiors of collapsing stars. The carbon dioxide you exhale on every breath came from planetary nebulas. Your connection to nature and to the earth (*Gaia*) as a whole is innate and symbiotic. You are the earth quantized and particularized as you. (See *Gaia Consciousness* reference.)

Egocentrism

Your egocentric consciousness is the product of the illusions it spins. It's built entirely on the misconceptions through the misperceptions it weaves. Its path turns out to be a cul-de-sac of delusion and despair.

Don't let an unenlightened ego get in your way. If it becomes too inflated, let it go. Your hot air will lift it into an atmosphere that knows how to deflate it.

The Tibetan word for ego is *dak dzin*. *Dak* means 'self' and *dzin* 'to grasp.' When put together it means 'grasping at self.' In particular, the teachings say that dak dzin refers to 'grasping at' or 'identifying with' a false sense of self. That pretty much describes our warped egocentric nature.

Egoic Lotus

The three tiers of petals (knowledge, love and sacrifice) that open over the immense period of time that constitutes your quantum soul journey are known as the egoic lotus. Eventually, the three petals of the central bud (the jewel in the lotus) are opened when you achieve total and complete *Self-Realization.*

The Elsewhere

There's an intuitive sense of spacetime, stemming from your super-conscious awareness, that tells you there's an 'everywhere else' beyond your normal egocentric awareness and an indefinable 'elsewhere' when it comes to your flesh-and-blood human experiences. This infinite 'elsewhereness' seems to have no known causal connection with your own finite 'space.' Upon reflection, you'll get a sense that it extends beyond your conceptual ability - and perhaps your believability horizons. Yet, you have a strong sense it's there whether you call it heaven, extra-dimensional beingness, purgatory, or hell. Perhaps you have this 'elsewhere' sensitivity because you've been there—and know what it's like before you chose the limitations associated with another skin school experience!

Embedded Theology

I invite you to get out of bed with the embedded religious theology you've spent soooooo much of your time with, so the bed bugs (dogma, errant edited scripture, the concept of an anthropomorphic god meme, an exclusive mindset, etc.) won't bite.

In my youth and early adulthood I'd been on a 'life-support system' (mainstream Christianity) that turned out to be a 'meaningful life aborted system.' So, I chose an unplugged perspective (MetaSpirituality) because there's an lot more philosophical, metaphysical and scientific elbow room out there.

Endless Punishment

You mindlessly create and perpetuate endless punishment when you fail to align your human self with your Divine Nature (*Logos Nature*).

Enlightenment

An enlightened perspective means you do not have to depend on external events as the foundations of your superior spiritual discernment or as the basis for your deeper, more esoteric understanding. And you certainly don't need the world of outer appearances to serve as the footing for your advanced metaphysical beliefs and guiding principles. Because you're divinely ordering your earth experiences using your heightened spiritual awareness, you'll no longer base your thoughts, intentions, choices and actions on the unenlightened worldly whims of your egocentric consciousness.

Breathe in and then breathe out. Inhale and now exhale. If you neglect to do this, any concerns about your enlightenment, or the best prayer technique to use, or the right church or synagogue to attend, or which password to use for your online banking will be the least of your problems.

When it comes to wanting to become more enlightened, don't suffer from a pain in the ask! Ask for guidance. Seek direction. Inquire about spiritual teachings and paths to explore. Examine the efficacy of various spiritual practices. Question all unquestioned answers. Call upon your inner Guidance and Wisdom (*vidya*).

There are no elevators or escalators to enlightenment. You'll need to use the rungs in Jacob's Ladder. (See the Jacob's Ladder reference in our book entitled *More Straight Talk About Spiritual Stuff*)

Unless you commit to your own enlightenment (aligning your small 's' self with your capital 'S' *Self*), others will only be able to offer you detours, side trips, blind alleys, false promises, and running in place.

Think about the 'big' successes you'll be able to achieve when you're enlightened while you're enjoying the 'small' successes now, so all your small successes go in the right direction.

Entering the Stream

Stepping into a stream or river symbolically means intentional and disciplined Self-Unification (Self-Alignment), affording us the opportunity to enjoy being in the 'flow' of life-affirming currents of higher spiritual thought as we unite consciously with our Higher Spiritual Self. In Buddhism, truth seekers (initiates) who enter the first degree of initiation are called *sotapattis* or *sohans,* which mean 'one who has entered the stream.' In Hinduism these initiates are called *parivrajakas* which means 'wanderers.'

Epistemic Ethics

A spiritual teacher has epistemic authority when making declarative truth statements that students presume are reliable knowledge and appropriate, and yet, students who are not quite spiritually attuned may feel no obligation to accept or apply the teachings.

Spiritual teachers have been saddled with this dilemma for centuries. Truth practitioners must raise the octave of their consciousness to a level of spiritual understanding that realizes that it is not the consequences of actions that make actions right or wrong, but the motives of the person who carries out the action. Nor is learning spiritual teachings enough. You must take action!

If you do not apply the spiritual principles you know,
you will not gain the traction needed
to achieve Self-Realization.

Errorville

Divinity-denying thoughts, intentions, inclinations, choices, words and actions that impede, limit or detour your Self-Realization are all components of errorville.

A stone in your shoe, a bug in your ear, a spec of dust in your eye, a splinter in your foot, a bout with stomach flu, and a quarrel with your family are nothing compared to your divinity-denying thoughts, words and actions.

Esoteric Perspective

Esoteric views (metaphysical views, metaphorical views, figurative views, analogical views) of reality are views limited by your level of awareness. Wouldn't you agree? There's no *"the view"* of reality because humankind hasn't progressed to the highest level of super-enlightened awareness (if there is a highest level). We're all unfolding in a sea of consciousness which is universal and unlimited.

In the ultimate science of 'being awakened' you come to realize that there is only One Reality (One Consciousness. One Substance, One Presence, the All, One Universal Mindlikeness, etc.) and all ideas, self-knowledge, and higher understanding are aspects of that Pure Universal Consciousness. If you do not understand that, you must re-think (repent) your own level of intellectual Bodhi. Forgetting who you are will lead to your losing many opportunities to receive deeper metaphysical insights, because such esoteric guidance comes unexpectedly and is usually short-lived ("you will not know what hour I come" say the scriptures of many faith traditions) unless you study it and apply it conscientiously.

Essenes

The more cosmic notion of the Logos principle is believed to have been espoused by the Essenes (2nd century BCE), who were an esoteric Jewish sect. The Essenes had extensive cosmic knowledge, and may have gotten the concept of the Logos from Heraclitus of Ephesus (550-480 BCE). Also, there seems to be a direct link between the disciple Matthew and the Essenes. Matthew was evidently a pupil of Matthai (who was a follower of Jeshu ben Pandira, founder of the Essene movement). As a matter of fact, a large number of Matthew's writings echo Essene teachings so much that Rudolf Steiner and others refer to the Gospel of Matthew as the 'Gospel of the Essenes.' (See Logos reference.)

Ethereal Body (Vital Body, Cosmic Intermediary)

The energetic counterpart (ethereal foundation) of your physical body, which is composed of seven major centers (chakras) and 49, or more, minor centers. It's a network which connects all the centers, and infinitesimally small threads of energy (*nadis*) which underlie every part of your nervous system. Blockages in the Etheric Body usually result in physical illnesses.

Etherealization

Etherealization is the stage in your mature spiritual growth (*Self-Realization*) when you dispense with your physical envelope and your Ethereal Body becomes your lowest envelope of being. This is the New Jerusalem (your Zohar Body, your *Universal Self Actualized Spiritual Body*) the Bible talks about. (See our book entitled *The Book of Revelation: New Metaphysical Version.*)

Eve

Eve symbolizes superior intuition and your potential to *feeeeel* and expresss your feelings about sensory experience in skin school. For example, the 'conversation' between 'Eve and the serpent' is the dialogue going on in your head as you try to summon the courage to awaken the kundalini energies within on your quest for enlightenment.

Eve's fear of 'dying' is the same cautionary emotion all of us experience when we realize that the kundalini's rise from our Root Chakra to our Crown Chakra means the subordination of our ego —and all of its sensory attachments—to our *Divine Nature*, our *True Nature.*

Everlasting Hell

Remaining in a hellish state of consciousness by refusing to acknowledge your innate divinity and the innate divinity of others is essentially being in a state of everlasting hell. One of these days we'll prefer a heavenly state of consciousness even though, initially, it may be a bit lonely 'at the top,' instead of staying in a hellish state of consciousness just for the company. Fellowship is a good thing unless it keeps you in a shallowship of unenlightened company.

The 'seven deadly sins' are the chief cocktails in a hellish state of consciousness. By analogy, they could also be the refusal, or laziness, or disinterest, or lethargy, neglectfulness, or indifference, or apathy to actualize none of the seven major chakras which lead to your enlightenment.

Hellions are simply hellish thoughts, atrocious words, damnable choices, and diabolical actions.

Your thinking can take you to heaven (a blissful, peaceful and loving state of consciousness) or hell (an savagely hurtful, barbaric, monstrous state of consciousness).

Evil

Evil—like any other wicked, foul, corrupt, immoral, malevolent thought, word or action—is one of the forms of error in physicality (the relative world). At the level of Spirit there is no evil, because the Pure Universal Consciousness epitomizes all that is good, perfect, sacred and pure in the Absolute Realm. Pure Universal Consciousness (God, One Reality, etc.) underwrites all that exists in physicality (Its relative aspect), so that mutations (errors and evils) like those I mentioned above that occur are the effects of a divinity-denying consciousness that represses its inherent goodness. The goodness is there, and will always be there; however, sentient and insentient beings alike, will have to realign themselves with the goodness which is their True Nature in order to expiate (rectify, absolve, remedy) the error(s) they've set into motion.

Exclusivity

Exclusivity is a 'bye product' of a religious fundamentalist mindset. It says "Good-bye" to human decency, unconditional love and compassion.

Experiences

The nature of gentle rains and a nurturing sun is the same, and yet both thorns and flowers grow in the same garden.

ॐ   ॐ   ॐ

Fairy Tales

The deceitful falsehoods, myths, misrepresentations, out-and-out lies, smoke and mirrors, ridiculous concoctions, delusions, fictitious monstrosities, unbelievable hallucinations, pretentious baloney, and whoppers the unenlightened ego tells in every waking moment are the fairy tales humankind has bought into for centuries.

Faith

Believing even when we have not seen—that's faith. But I think it's really important to recognize that faith is a powerful spiritual perspective which we can develop and grow. People are prone criticize themselves when it appears they don't have the faith they think they should, and beat themselves up. From a MetaSpiritual perspective, faith is trust in action—trust in your ability as a spiritual being to divinely order good regardless of the pull of outer appearances.

As you move forward on your spiritual journey, recognize it is a process of growing and developing your Faith Quotient—'Faithing it till you make it' through practice: affirming the Truth of what you know, denying doubt any power, moving forward claiming the good that is yours by right of consciousness! And become more aware of your divine genealogy! Bless the inflow and outflow of everything in your life, knowing that goodness underwrites all physical manifestation.

Faith is not clinging to belief or hope, it's releasing any and all doubts, fears, vacillation and disquiet in the unfailing alignment (oneing) of your human self with your Divine Nature.

The placebic power of faith is awesome!

Fallibilistic Knowledge

This perspective holds that absolute certainty about knowledge is impossible. It admits that because empirical knowledge is oftentimes revised by further study and observation, all knowledge, except that which is axiomatically true exists in a constant state of flux.

The Fall

The 'Fall' is a religious concept mainstream religious communities have sold us for centuries. In my opinion, there was no 'Fall.' What has been referred to as 'the Fall' is simply—and I mean simply—our decision as spiritual beings to pursue (continue, actualize) our *Self-Realization* by assuming human form on this Earth plane and/or assuming a complementary form in another dimension of being. And because I believe there was no 'fall,' there was no 'original sin,' and there is no need to be rescued by anyone or anything who was – or should be - sacrificed for our 'sins.' (See an additional Fall reference in our *More Straight Talk* book.)

The 'fall,' original sin, the need for atonement, the belittling and subjugation of women, the inerrancy of scripture, the virgin birth, the insistence on a literal-only interpretation of scripture, and final Judgment Day, are a few of the many claims made by a barbaric theology! (See the Barbaric Theology reference.)

In 'crossover' MetaSpiritual/quantum physics terms, as spiritual beings who have chosen a human experience, we have settled for limitation (particulate form, physical incarnation, matter, mass) over limitlessness (wave form, spiritual unboundedness, timeless etherealness).

Fallen Angels

Metaphysically, fallen angels are spiritual thoughts that degrade into purely materialistic thoughts.

Fasting

If you're going to fast, I invite you to *fast* from any fears you may have about losing your job or finding a new one in this Prosac economy. If you're going to *abstain* from anything, *abstain* from the belief that you aren't meant to have more or that you'll never be prosperous. If you're going to *renounce* anything, *renounce* the 'worship' of a deity in the sky and claim your 'worthship' as the human expression of the One reality.

Fasting from outdated assumptions and perspectives that denigrate you and cause you to doubt your worth is the message I'd like to share.

Cher's and my perspective on *fasting* is simple. We advocate fasting from those toxic thoughts, beliefs, and attitudes that characterize an external locus of control! A few examples of those kinds of toxic thoughts, beliefs, attitudes, and actions are: belief in luck or fate; a bias for negativity; feelings of helplessness; labeling oneself as a victim; placing blame on other people, things, or circumstances; believing you're unworthy; being fooled by the world of appearances.

Field of Infinite Being

For conversation's sake, imagine arcing your arms in front of you and spreading them into as wide a circle as you can. Imagine this represents the expansiveness, the limitlessness, the universality, the eternality of Pure Universal Consciousness. Then imagine the *Field of Infinite Being* enveloping the same space. The 'Field' is limitless, without boundaries, and eternal, too. It is Pure Universal Consciousness (the Übermind, the Eternal Presence, God, Brahman, the Infinite Isness, Absolute Good, or one of the 72,000 names humankind has attributed to that 'Something' that is the Ground of All Being) expressing as the *Field*! Within the *Field of Infinite Being* are levels of consciousness interpenetrating each other and expanding exponentially at the same time.

Field Trips

Metaphysically speaking, an out-of-body experience; an incarnational or reincarnational experience; astral travel; giving cognitive dissonance a chance; a guided meditation; journeying into your subconsciousness; a mystical experience, etc., are all extrasensory field trips.

Fiery Furnace

Whenever we find ourselves in the fiery furnace of the world of appearance … feeling attacked by negativity, fear, lack, or anything else that threatens to destroy our spirit, all you have to do is call on that age-old wisdom from firefighters which my brilliant wife, Cher, wordsmithed into a spiritual principle: "Stop – Drop – Roll!

STOP … and Recognize that what you are experiencing is not the Truth of who you are. **DROP** … any error thinking and behaviors that are contributing to the fiery emotional furnace you are experiencing. **ROLL** … with Truth principles, your metaphysical knowledge, and your connection with your Higher Spiritual Self." I like it when we cross-pollinate the languaging and expand interdisciplinary applications. Stop – Drop – Roll. Can you dig it!

First Born

A newly created divine idea 'birthing' into conscious awareness is a first born idea.

Five Physical Senses

Our five physical senses raised to their highest, most elevated interdimensional level are: clairvoyance, clairaudience, clairalience, clairsentience and clairgustance.

Flight Into Solitude

As we looked at where we are spiritually—allegorically, metaphysically, philosophically, and MetaSpiritually—and where the majority of humankind is in terms of its almost complete unawareness of its Divine Nature, Cher and I wondered how much difference we could make in helping the world awaken to its *True Spiritual Nature*. There have been many people (outliers), far superior to us in intellect and influential positions of authority who helped form the basis of our rarified spiritual perspective, but were themselves unable to ease humankind out of its slumber. Many of these outliers went into seclusion—or were forced into it, by a world society that refused to give up its entrenched dogma when it came to religious beliefs.

We, too, have thought about retreating into solitude to achieve *Self-Realization* without having to deal with the negativity and close-mindedness of a sleepwalking humanity. However, we have decided to avoid what St. Augustine described as the temptation of *fuga in solitudinem* (the flight into solitude). Instead, we will continue to openly share what we believe to be the sacred soul journey to humankind's collective enlightenment.

Forbidden Fruit

I believe the proverbial Biblical 'Forbidden Fruit' is the conglomeration of sensory pleasures and addictions associated with physicality itself. It's not an apple, or fig, or grape, or pomegranate, or carob (pea), or citron (citrus), or other fruit. Esoterically, the 'forbidden fruit' is believed to be a selfish inclination, or need for greed, or sensual appetite, or irrational passion, or the desire for pleasure, or even the lust for orgasm. Perhaps we could even add the need for bling, or the addiction to smart phones, or the craving for chocolate, or a fondness for fast cars! Whatever it was, this 'sensory fruit' tempts us to incarnate into physicality (the world of limitation) to experience all the sense-addictions that are associated with our yearning for skin school experiences.

Apart from the Earth plane hankering, the lust for the 'forbidden fruit' can also refer to the temptations you experience in any of your ethereal bodies which serve as your outer vehicles in other dimensions of being based on your accumulated karma, mental capacities and quantum world interests. One last comment. The 'forbidden fruit' seems to come from the Tree of the

Knowledge of Good (your *Self-Realized Divine Nature*) and Evil (your divinity-denying egocentric nature). So, it looks like we're talking about the 'Tree of Polarities.' And that leads me to reiterate my first statement: The forbidden fruit is physicality itself!

Forgiveness

The freedom of a simple act of forgiveness can offset the *feedom* generated by the high costs of hatred, resentment and anger. Forgiveness is not as difficult to prescribe as you might think. It's not a difficult thing—letting go of the struggle to protect your bruised, if not battered ego. It can be, of course; but you have the power to move past a victim mentality and into a victor consciousness that says, "I can master anything that happens to me down here in skin school!" Forgiveness is joyful, easy, up-lifting and freeing. I speak from my own experiences and can site hundreds of instances that show the therapeutic effects of well-timed forgiveness. Forgiveness is a powerful therapy. It is the antidote of all conflict-ridden interpersonal ailments. Metaphysically, forgiveness means giving up the false for the true. That means seeing the other person's true Divine Nature instead of his or her human frailties and shortcomings.

Four Lower Bodies

The four lower bodies are the sheaths of four distinct frequencies that surround the soul (your ego personality): the etheric, or memory body; the mental body; the desire, or emotional, body; and the physical body. The etheric body (Quantum Self) houses the blueprint of your soul's quantum identity and contains the memory of all that has ever transpired in your soul and all impulses you have ever experienced. The mental body is the vessel of your mindlike cognitive faculties. When purified, it can become the mindlike receptacle of your God Essence (the Eternal Presence, the One Reality that underwrites your physical being). Your desire body houses the higher and lower desires and records your emotions. The physical body is your 'leased' flesh and blood body that enables you to move about on the physical plane (skin school).

Fundamental Christianity

Whenever I'm around particularly vocal fundamental Christians, I feel as uneasy as the Tree of Life must feel standing near the dog dump area at a rest stop.

Mainstream, fundamentalist religion dunks you and holds your head down in the shallow end of the pool—and your own guilt, fear and shame keep you from standing up on your own two feet. I encourage you to dive into the deep end and get to the bottom of spiritual things.

ॐ   ॐ   ॐ

Gaia Consciousness

At the Gaiaic level of consciousness the atmosphere, the seas, the terrestrial crust are seen as the result of interventions carried out by Gaia, through the co-evolving diversity of all of its living organisms. Bioscientists and plant neurobiologists have known for years that our planet is a self-regulating ecosystem and that most of its life forms organize to contribute to the benefit of the whole. For example, plants can sense light (because they grow toward the sun and artificial light). They can 'smell' chemicals released by other plants which trigger specific reactions in the plant. Plants sense gravity and can even hear. I'm not kidding. I wouldn't 'plant' something like that on you without researching it.

In a fascinating experiment, researchers played the sound of a caterpillar munching on leaves to nearby plants - and the plants released defensive chemicals based on the sound alone. Isn't that incredible! Research has shown that plants have memories and even react to anesthetics. While tomatoes may not be able to scream, some plants emit compounds that warn their 'compatriots' of approaching threats - the botanical equivalent of a smoke signal. Neat huh!

The dieffenbachia, a common houseplant, contains idioblasts that fire barbed calcium oxalate crystals into the mouths of predators which release an enzyme analogous to reptilian venom. Some plants have opted to 'hire' mercenaries. Several species of South American and African acacia tree both house and feed aggressive ants. These industrious little soldiers make their barracks inside swollen thorns and feed off of food bodies produced by the plant especially for them. The ants savagely defend their benefactors against all comers, whether they're animal, vegetable, or fungus. The ants even snip off the foliage of any other plants that have the nerve to encroach upon their acacia's personal space. In experiments where the ant colonies were removed, the trees died.

Plants that are attacked by insect predators or subjected to stressful conditions such as drought or microbial infection warn other plants of the impending crises by releasing volatile organic compounds (VOCs), which cause physiological reactions in nearby plants. They increase concentrations of toxic compounds to ward off enemies, or they release compounds of their own that attract their enemy's predators. Plants also communicate through chemicals released by their roots and even via networks of fungal *symbionts* (organisms that cooperate symbiotically).

Plants react to the presence of water and 'feel' obstructions – and even sense possible obstructions - in their root systems. Although plants don't have nerve cells like we humans, they do have a system for sending electrical signals. They even produce neurotransmitters, like dopamine, serotonin and other chemicals the human brain uses to send signals. Plants are conscious expressions of Pure Universal Consciousness and are ecologically connected with other sentient beings.

Believe it or not, natural elements like water and rocks have Gaia Consciousness. The wetness of water (its ability to maintain contact with surfaces) is a consequence of intermolecular interactions, notably hydrogen bonding among nearby water molecules. At the microlevel rocks consist of an unimaginable number of atoms connected by springy chemical bonds, all jiggling around at sub-atomic rates that even our fastest supercomputer might envy. And they don't jiggle at random. The rock's innards 'connect' with the entire universe by means of the gravitational and electromagnetic signals it is continuously receiving. Such a system can be viewed as an all-purpose information processor, one whose inner dynamics mirror any sequence of mental states characteristic of our human brains.

According to integrated information scientists our entire ecosystem is wired for consciousness and is a conscious Gaia organism. This level of Pure Universal Beingness recognizes that the electrons, protons and neutrons making up our brains are no different from those making up the rest of the world. So the entire universe consists of 'conscious beings' no matter how inanimate they appear.

Gelassenheit

Gelassenheit is a German word that has many interpretations, but from a personhood perspective it generally means Self-surrender and the serenity that comes from Self-surrender, the resignation of the ego to your *Higher Spiritual Self*, yieldedness to your Divine Nature, subordinating your egocentric nature to your Divine Self, and self-abandonment that leads to *Self-Realization.*

Gethsemane

Gethsemane is an Aramaic term (*Gaḏ-Šmānê*) that means 'oil press.' It is in an olive tree grove near Jerusalem. Its name derives from the process of heating nuts or seeds so you can extract natural oils. MetaSpiritually, Gethsemane represents our struggle in skin school to align our human self with our Divine Nature (*Cosmic Logos* or *Cosmic Christ Nature*). The 'oil' that we produce is our enlightenment and *Self-Realization.*

Global Dementia

Mainstream religions suffer from what I call global dementia. They encourage their followers to forget who they really are. People who subscribe to literalist religious teachings are walking around in physical bodies thinking those flesh and blood vehicles are their true identities. They've forgotten that they're spiritual beings who have leased their bodies in order to travel from point 'a' to point 'b' in this physical dimension. They've repressed the truth that they're the physical actualizations, the somatic expressions of the One Reality they call God (Great I Am/Pure Universal Consciousness/One Reality/Infinite Isness, etc.).

Omnipresence, Omnipotence, Omniscience and Omniactivity are the only known quantum attributes of God (Eternal Presence, Pure Universal Consciousness, Eternal Divine Principle, Supreme Ultimate reality, Infinite Isness, the One, the Absolute, the Oversoul, Existence Itself, etc.). Light, energy and love are only attributes of this Pure Universal Consciousness which is presently beyond all definition, description, and comprehension. So, you see, the attributes of anything—the rigid hardness of rocks, the heat of fire, the wetness and fluidity of water, the brisk gusts of air—are not the thing itself, just as a map is not the territory. Perhaps one day we'll discover that God causes omnipresence, omnipotence, omniscience, omniactivity, love, energy and light. These attributes do not describe the totality of God. They are expressions of God's Godness.

You are the 'Great I Am' (the One Reality, God)
particularized as you.

Although there's no geography in Spirit there can be plenty of cognitive 'distance' in our awareness of our God essence.

You're the Eternal Presence (God, the Great I Am, Pure Universal Consciousness) 'outposted' as you in human form.

In esoteric Hinduism, Pure Universal Consciousness is Brahman or Parabrahman. In esoteric Buddhism, it's Adi-Buddha or Adi-Buddhi meaning literally 'Primordial Wisdom' (vidya) while the Kabbalah uses the term Ein-Soph (also written as Ain-Soph) which literally means 'The Endless Boundless No-Thing.'

Everyday, in each day's experience, learn to
view your life from your God Essence,
which is the truth of who you are.

The cosmic presence and galactic power of the One Reality don't depend on our limited understanding and awareness of the nature of things. There's much more 'God stuff' for us to learn and experience.

Those who look outside for an anthropomorphic God meme in the sky dream, those who look inside their own beingness are awakened.

Gospel Writers

Biblical scholars aren't sure, to this day, who wrote the Gospels. However, two are believed to be named after two of Yeshua's (Jesus') disciples and two are attributed to companions of Peter and Paul respectively. Matthew is thought to be named after Matthew and John is ascribed to John, both were Jesus' apostles. Mark is named after a close friend and traveling companion of Peter and Luke after a traveling gentile buddy of Paul. If you've been taught any differently, you're not alone. But what I have just shared is based on the best critical Biblical scholarship we have to date! The inconvenient truth is these four people were almost certainly not the authors of the Gospels! There's no evidence to prove they were. I'm being absolutely straight with you!

Grace

When you move from an error thought, word or action by upping your thoughts, words and actions to a spiritual level, you've found grace. When you have a spiritual thought you've found grace. Every time you make a spiritually-attuned choice you've found grace. Each *Self-Realized a*ction you take is grace-full.

Gray Spirituality

A spiritual perspective that hasn't lost its dogmatic ties to a particular mainstream religious tradition, but seeks to rid itself of those organized ties by attempting to adopt more spiritual than religious practices and outlooks is what I call gray spirituality.

The Great Commission

According to mainstream Christian teachings, the 'Great Commission' is the instruction the resurrected Jesus (Yeshua) gave to his disciples to spread his teachings to all nations. And Jesus came and said to them, "All authority in heaven and on earth has been given to me. Go therefore and make disciples of all nations, baptizing them in the name of the Father and of the Son and of the Holy Spirit, teaching them to observe all that I have commanded you. And behold, I am with you always, to the end of the age."

The most familiar version came from Matthew's gospel (28:16-20). However, there were five other versions: Mark 16:14-18; Luke 24:44-49; John 20:19-23; Acts 1:4-8; and Romans 16:25-26.

I believe a MetaSpiritual interpretation makes the 'Great Commission' not just the disciples' commission, but every human being's commission. Here's my MetaSpiritual perspective: 17. We still may have some doubts as to our worthiness, 18. But we must remember that we are truly individualized expressions of Pure Universal Consciousness at the point of us. 19 And because that is the truth of us, we can literally transform our body, mind and soul (nations) by divinely ordering our experiences from the perspective of our *Self Consciousness* (in the name of the Father, Son, and Holy Spirit); 20. And because that clearly is the truth of us, we must spend every waking moment walking the path on faithful, loving and practical feet. We must purposefully and joyfully unfold toward our *Self-Realization,* remembering the eternal Omnipresence, Omnipotence, Omniscience and Omni-activity of our own I-Amness. There's much to do to raise the spiritual consciousness of the planet, as we add our own elevated spiritual awareness to the *Self-Realized* awareness of Yeshua (Jesus) and others who have attained *Selfhood.*

Great Flood

The Biblical *Great Flood* symbolizes the tsunamic sensory overload of self-negating thoughts, inclinations, choices, habits and behaviors that can destroy us with their divinity-denying nature that refuses to accept our status as human expressions of the Eternal

Presence. Flood myths abound in world scriptures and these motifs generally tell the same story. They're filled with enough poetic license to, well, flood the world's literature with a deluge of spectacular intrigue.

Great White Brotherhood

The Great White Brotherhood is a spiritual order of Western saints and Eastern adepts who shepherd humankind through its collective soul journey. They have transcended the cycles of karma and rebirth and ascended (accelerated) into that higher reality that is the eternal abode of enlightened souls. The ascended masters (adepts) of the Great White Brotherhood have risen in every age from every culture and religion to inspire creative achievement in education, the arts and sciences, government, and global goodwill. It's important for you to know that the word 'white' does not refer to race, but to the aura (halo) of white light that surrounds their ethereal forms.

ॐ   ॐ   ॐ

Happiness

Choose happiness, inner peace, joy, positivity and optimism, cheerfulness and laughter. Misery, gloom, worry, melancholy, pessimism, and bitterness are optional.

The search for happiness like the search for the approval of an anthropomorphic god 'out there' and anything else external to you will not bring you the happiness and inner peace you want, because what brings you fulfillment and meaning comes from within you.

Health and Healing

Conscious alignment (oneing) with your *Higher Spiritual Self* will provide you with much more than spiritual attunement. The closer your conscious alignment (oneing) is with your *True Spiritual Nature* the closer your physical body's connection will be with the species-specific *prana* (Qi attractor) that improves your capacity to resist illness and disease.

Throwing *pearls to swine,* in a MetaSpiritual context, is quite different from the one that you've heard in most religious explanations of that phrase. In my opinion, it can be interpreted from a positive, health-related perspective. I intuited this interpretation the week after my open heart surgery. Here's my retake on the *pearls* to swine Biblical reference: Creating superior medical technology (pearls) to provide technologically perfect tissue valves (swine) which are used in heart valve replacements, is a way of transforming a positive-to-negative Biblical connotation into a positive-to-positive orientation. There are many levels of Biblical and scriptural interpretation, many perspectives, many shades of meaning in everything we think, do, and say.

I invite you to turn heeling into healing every chance you get.

Helicopter God

We don't want to sound like overprotective ministers who hover over your every move, but Cher and I invite you to let the concept of a helicopter God meme (a drone God in today's parlance) flutter out of your consciousness. There never has been a helicopter (drone) God. It's the fig newton of a patriarchal, old school, religious mindset. A helicopter God (anthropomorphic God meme, drone God) is the foundation of mainstream religious traditions around the world. It has been reinforced through mistranslated and misinterpreted scriptures, perpetuated by fossilized doctrinal edicts, and preserved by millions of well-intentioned—although unenlightened—ministers in pulpits throughout America and beyond.

Heptaparaparshinokh

According to Gurdjieff, who coined the term *'sacred Heptaparaparshinokh,'* it is the patterning principle of divinely ordering our experience. Gurdjieff believes our thinking process involves seven phases: *perception* (of something desired), *understanding, thought, judgment, choice, will*, and *determination towards some kind of action* (the fruits of our labor).

Psychologists have linked the thinking process with Piaget's developmental stages (sensory motor, pre-operational, concrete operational and formal operational) and organized phases of thinking that are characteristic with each developmental stage. Psychologists have also added perceptual, conceptual, reflective, conjecture, abstract, hypothetical, propositional, syllogistic, and creative thinking which are defined by their own processes.

Hidden Cities

MetaSpiritually, hidden cities are the pockets of Self-limiting awareness and debilitating patterns of self-negation that are housed in our subconsciousness from incarnation to incarnation.

Hidden Manna

MetaSpiritually speaking, hidden manna is the spiritual insights, revelations, ideas and epiphanies, intuitions and feelings of bliss, joy, serenity, and tranquility that epitomize your conscious oneness with the One Reality many people call God. It's these forms of manna that are your soul food.

This hidden manna comes from your super-consciousness as a result of transformational *insperiences* like sitting meditation, mystical experiences and visualizations. (Discover more Hidden Manna in our *Life-Changing Spiritual Practices, Volumes 1-10,*and on our website, TheGlobalCenterForSpiritualAwakening.com)

Higher Spiritual Self

Your *Higher Spiritual Self* is your *Cosmic Logos Nature*. It's the One Reality (Eternal Presence, Pure Universal Consciousness, etc.) expressing Itself through Its *Cosmic Logos Nature* as you.

It's not so much that your Higher Spiritual Self is within you as you are within It.

Holons

In physics, holons are made up of their own parts, yet are part of a larger whole. Human beings are quantum holons, and so are cities, communities, nations, and ecosystems. For example, as far as machines are concerned, a machine (the whole) equals the sum of its parts. If a machine malfunctions, the cause is attributed to one of its parts. When it comes to human beings (quantum holons) the whole is greater than the sum of its parts. So, healing a particular part will not necessarily cure the whole person. The whole person (the transcendental, spiritual you) will have to be realized as a whole through persistent alignment on your part for there to be complete wellness (enlightened wholeness).

How 'Yeshua' Became 'Jesus'

Yeshua is the Hebrew name, and its English spelling is 'Joshua.' *Iesous* is the Greek transliteration (the sound of the name) of the Hebrew name, and its English spelling is 'Jesus.' Some people say that calling Yeshua 'Jesus' is blasphemous. Other scholars acknowledge that the name 'Jesus' is unbiblical because the letter 'J' is a modern invention since there was no letter J in Greek or Hebrew alphabets. When you think about it, that's why no one in Yeshua's day would have accurately pronounced the English name *Jesus*. Mainstream Christians refer to Yeshua as 'Jesus' because that's the only name they've been taught.

Suppose you went back in time to meet the twelve apostles and asked Peter to "take you to see *Jesus Christ.*" You would probably see a puzzled look migrate across his face and hear him ask the equivalent of, "Who or what is that?" He would not have connected the Greek transliteration of Yeshua or its English pronunciation. He wouldn't have known to whom or what you were referring. Why? Because the sound the letter 'J' makes has never existed in the Hebrew, Aramaic, Greek or Latin languages.

When the angel Gabriel came to Mary and told her she was going to have a son and that the child's name was to be 'Yehoshua,' it was the blending of two Hebrew words: The first part, 'Yeh-ho,' is part of Yahweh's name that is sometimes used at the beginning or end of Hebrew names. The second part of Yehoshua's name, 'shua,' is the Hebrew word for 'saves or deliverance.' The name 'Yehoshua' literally means *God saves*. The name *Yehoshua* was then shortened to Yeshua.

Around 400 C.E. the Latin language became the predominate language of Christianity and the Greek versions of the New Testament were translated into Latin. The Latin Bible (*Vulgate*) transliterated what was left of Yeshua's Greek name by sounding it out as 'ee-ay-soos.' The new transliteration of the Greek name 'ee-ay-soos' became written as 'Iesus' and was identical in pronunciation to the Greek name. This Latin spelling and on-going transliteration dominated the Christian world for the next 1, 000 years.

In 1384 John Wycliffe translated the *New Testament* to English for the first time. His only source was the Latin Vulgate. Wycliffe continued to use the Latin spelling and pronunciation of Iesus. The printing press had not yet been invented until Gutenberg invented it in the 1450's. Then, in 1526, William Tyndale was the first to use the letter 'J' in spelling the name 'Jesus.'

Human Egocentric Consciousness

A growing number of neuroscientists are beginning to believe that the portal between our brain and our mind is housed biologically in the claustrum, which is the physical control center that determines how conscious and connected we are with Pure Universal Consciousness. Our brain simply registers and records the levels of conscious interconnectivity and activity with our surroundings—not just on planet Earth but inter-dimensionally with what quantum physicists call parallel universes.

We humans can experience many states of consciousness: nocturnal dreaming and daydreaming, hypnopompic and hypnogogic hallucinatory states, meditative states, trance states, drug induced states, hypnotic states, comatose and regressive states, mystical and rapturous states, out-of-body states, 'normal' waking state, super-conscious states (poltergeist activity, materializations and dematerializations, teleportation, and levitation), the quantum conscious state, etc.

Spiritually speaking, there is one state of consciousness at this level of consciousness that has given us the most trouble—the consciousness of separation from the Pure Universal Beingness (God, Brahman, the Eternal Presence, etc.) that expresses Itself as us and everything else. It's that consciousness of assumed separation from our God essence that triggers our repeated reincarnations and incarnations.

Human Genome Book of Life, Karma and the Kangyur

The *Human Genome Book of Life* is massive and contains 24 chapters which outline the 3 billion base pairs of the human genome, organized into 24 distinct microscopic genome units. That makes over 100,000 genes in our DNA. Each of these chapters is written in a long chain of DNA in a series of four letters (A,C,G and T). We can strike a comparison between the *Human Genome Book of Life* to the Tibetan Buddhist *Kangyur* (Translated Words) which consists of treatises in 108 volumes supposed to have been spoken by the Buddha himself: Imagine that during the thousands of years of copying the *Kangyur* treatises, that every now and then small scribal errors occurred. These errors were probably perpetuated in subsequent copying, which created copying variations.

Some of the smaller variations may not have had a noticeable impact on the integrity of the copy. However, sometimes major variations occurred that had far-reaching consequences which tainted the original meaning of a treatise (much like a mutation in a human gene would cause in our biological makeup). By analogy, this would help to explain how 'karmic mutations' over several lifetimes could affect our current genome, producing personality and physical anomalies that seem uncharacteristic of us in our current incarnation and, perhaps, a bit unfair, since the cause of our suffering doesn't appear to be something we initiated in our present skin school experience. (See Biblical Literalist Memories Questioned reference.)

Humility

Humility is not necessarily thinking less of yourself, or that you're unworthy. Nor is it devaluing the contributions you've made and can make. But it's thinking more of yourself less in order to leave room for thinking of the welfare of others more.

Hylozoic Universe

One day we'll discover that the universe truly is hylozoic (all matter has life and is conscious matter). What if the atoms and molecules that make up things—and the things themselves, regardless of their supposed inanimate nature—really are conscious beings with souls? That makes sense to me. How 'bout you?

Hypertime Drive

Hypertime is the speed of consciousness which is a gazillion times faster than the speed of light. You engage your hypertime drive every time you 'up your consciousness' (raise your awareness) to a super-conscious level.

Hypocrite

An egocentric thought, spoken word or action that cons its way into your conscious awareness pretending to be a product of your divine nature, but is laced with the phoniness of the masquerading ego. Actually, any error thought, word, choice or action that is produced by us is a hypocrite, because it's not congruent with our True Spiritual Nature (we are spiritual beings having a human experience).

ॐ   ॐ   ॐ

Identity

Ask yourself the four 'W's: *Where* are you when you're not yourself? *Who* are you when you're not yourself? *What* are you when you're not yourself? *When* are you when you're not yourself?

According to the best minds in neuroscience, there are no neuro-receptors that distinguish gradations of gray. Spiritually speaking, we must come to realize that there is no gray area when it comes to accepting our divine nature.

If you feel you are disconnected from your *Extraordinary Nature (Divine Nature, Higher Spiritual Nature)*, you may want to apply the **SIFI test**. Ask yourself these questions:

- S = *Spiritual Practice* (Am I making time for it on a regular basis?);
- I = *Inner Voice* (Does my self-talk need to be edited?);
- F = *Forgiveness* (Is there forgiveness work to be done?);
- I = *Inner Peace* (Am I allowing myself to breath easily and be present to the now moment?).

From *Cognito ergo sum* (I think, therefore I am) to *Credo ergo sum* (I believe, therefore I am) to *Ergo sum ergo* (I am, therefore I am).

When you leave this vibration called the physical you (human you), you'll move on as another impermanent version of you in another dimension of being. How long you remain as the next version of you depends on your level of awareness and your purposefulness in that particular dimension of being. Your consciousness determines your beingness (your denseness or airiness, ephemeralness or enduringness, quantumness or etherealness).

You must deny the denial of your innate divinity.

Your current 'self' is but a quantum phase of your *'Eternal Self,'* much like a wave – large or small, lengthy or abbreviated – is merely an aspect of an ocean. Both the 'self' and the 'wave' are conditional states of being. Each enjoys a span of temporal beingness before it returns to its greater, more transcendent beingness.

How much of you are you willing to release before you allow yourself to discover the *Real You?*

From the perspective of consciousness, the difference between us humans, animals, fowl, insects, plants and rocks is a matter of the heuristics of our unfoldment and karmic interconnectedness with other sentient, as well as insentient beings in this entangled cosmos. Even the laws (scientific perspectives) of quantum physics are intricately entangled with the karma of the conscious beings that arise in that universe (dimension, Megaverse, multiverse).

According to physicist Carl von Weizsäcker and a growing number of quantum physicists, we must abolish, once and for all, the separability of subject and object. That reasoning doesn't just apply to quantum physicists and their conception of our relationship with the universe. It applies to our conception of our relationship as quantum aspects of the One Reality called by many names. Humankind must outgrow the separability of our indivisible relationship with the One Reality (subject) which supposedly observes us, the supposedly observed (object). MetaSpiritually, there's no subject-object because we're indivisibly one with the One Reality. We're Its human expressions and It's our Universal Cosmic Source.

Ill Society

I encourage you to acknowledge, but not accept, an ill society that professes humanitarian interests, but fails to act on those interests. Humankind must move beyond its penchant to accept violence, wars, abuses of all kinds, over-consumption, destructive addictions, all forms of divisiveness and corruption, hate and shame in all of their forms, world hunger, damaging the environment, etc. Once we acknowledge that these things exist, we must collectively remedy them and their ill effects. Millions of enlightened people are already doing this. I invite you to add your consciousness and humanitarian interests to theirs.

Imagination

Imagination takes us beyond the fringe of egocentrism and into the depths of our super-consciousness.

Imitation

Acquiring knowledge is a form of imitation if it becomes an end in itself and copied, instead of a means to deepen your own understanding and expanded awareness. That's why I don't 'guru worship.' Being tethered to a guru is putting your *Self Expression* on hold. Imitating a guru's knowledge and adopting it as your own, leaves you stuck in his or her limited understanding and puts what you know in the frozen context of the guru's level of enlightenment.

I've never been a fan of 'one channel' religion or one perspective guruship. A river can't flow with only one bank.

Immaculate Conception

You create an immaculate conception every time you blend the divinely inspired result of your intuitive intelligence, love, and receptivity to your innate divinity by raising these spiritual qualities to their highest and purest alchemical essences so that you immaculately conceive a pure, inviolate Divine Idea. When you do this, the vibration of every atom, cell and molecule within your body is raised to its alchemical perfection by the virgin surge of highly spiritualized energies that lift you into a 'new' state of being. You literally 'birth' yourself into a holier abiding place (higher order of being) for your Divine Nature to 'live.'

Indecent Composure

Calmly professing that you believe in an anthropomorphic, white-bearded god meme in the sky—with a straight face, is a form of indecent composure.

Infinity's Incalcuability

Infinity squared is incalculable because infinity is incalculable. That may seem like a 'duh,' but attempting to measure the immeasurable is not only confusing activity with accomplishment, it's trying to set limits on limitlessness so we can grasp what infinity is. It's letting the limits of our conscious awareness define the measurement systems we use to understand the immeasurable. In Buddhism, there is an acknowledgment of the practical impossibility of trying to comprehend infinity. That rabbit hole is described in a chapter of the Buddha's *Flower Ornament Scripture* entitled 'The Incalculable.'

To penetrate the meaning of infinite world systems and the limits of human knowledge, he uses a string of calculations of mindboggling numbers. He instructs, "Ten to the tenth power times ten to the tenth power equals ten to the twentieth power; ten to the twentieth power times ten to the twentieth power equals ten to the fortieth power; ten to the fortieth power times ten to the fortieth power equals ten to the eightieth power." and on and on until he arrives at … "the previous number squared is ten to the power of 101, 493, 392, 610, 318, 652, 755, 325, 638, 410, 240. He calls that number squared an 'incalculable.' For me, the 'incalculable' goes both ways: How infinite is infinite and how finite is finite? What's the square root of finiteness?

Inflow of Illumination

The inflow of illumination into your super-consciousness is artesian-like. All you have to do is open up your receptivity to allow the light to shine in the darkness of your egocentric nature.

Innatistic Entry

Innatistic entries are incarnational and reincarnational experiences which happen to all of us who enter into skin school. Because we have been here before (reincarnation) or have come from another dimension and are here for the first time (incarnation) we are not blank slates as was commonly believed. We come here with prior extra-dimensional karmic experiences and knowledge.

Inner Prompting

In 2005 I got a strong inner prompting—actually, the 'Still Small Voice yelled! It wasn't the proverbial calling from an anthropomorphic deity (which doesn't – and never has existed, in my opinion), but an intense inner prompting to deepen my spirituality through the Unity Movement's ordination process to become a New Thought minister. My beautiful wife, Cher, felt the same intense inner prompting from her Higher Spiritual Self at the same time I felt mine. We do a lot of things together and the synchronicity of our life journeys continues to amaze us.

I mention this because, although we are proud of our Unity credentialing, we have expanded the bandwidth of our spiritual perspective soooo much that we have gained the reputation of being loveable, but rebellious, Unity ministers. We're not even mainstream Unity anymore! Our message is not a one-channel message (espousing a Unity-only spiritual perspective based on Unity's co-founders). Our message is a MetaSpiritual perspective that places the Trojan Horses of science and metaphysics in the Troy of mainstream—and New Thought—religious traditions.

Inner Sun

The Inner Sun the mystics talk about is our Higher Spiritual Nature (our Logos Nature) and the interior moon is our human personality which derives its light from the Inner Sun. When we deny our innate divinity we create a solar eclipse of the Inner Sun which prolongs our *Self-Realization*.

INRI

The acronym INRI (*Iēsus Nazarēnus, Rēx Iūdaeōrum*) stands for the Latin inscription used to identify the *Cosmic Logos* as Jesus which in English reads as 'Jesus the Nazarene, King of the Jews.' And the *Gospel of John* states that this inscription was written in three languages, Hebrew, Latin, and Greek, during the crucifixion of Yeshua (Jesus). There are esoteric meanings of INRI and the following two are Cher's and my favorites:

Ignis Natura Renovatur Integram—Fire Unceasingly Renews Nature.

In Necis Renascor Integer—In Death I Am Reborn Intact and Pure.

The first esoteric meaning of INRI, *Ignis Natura Renovatur Integra* (Fire Renews Nature Incessantly or Fire Unceasingly Renews Nature) refers to the universal cosmic solar fire of the Eternal Presence. It's the cosmic fire (Pure Universal Consciousness) that underwrites all that is, including our ethereal Vital Body, and in order to become illumined, we must manifest Its power through the crucifixion experience (the process of crossing out error). The crucifixion cosmically represents the purifying dynamics of the Universal Flame, but in us it represents INRI (the cleansing and purifying inner fire that we need to awaken to become fully enlightened).

Our second esoteric favorite, *In Necis Renascor Integer* (In Death I Am Reborn Intact and Pure or To Be Reborn, Through Mystical Death, Intact and Pure), has to do with the raw material, the crucible of physicality itself. Physicality itself, when you think about it, is the cross we must bear as spiritual beings who have chosen a human experience on the Earth plane and/or a humanlike (intelligent being) experience in another dimension of being.

So, in higher order thinking "in death I am reborn" refers to subordinating our egocentric consciousness (dying to the need for sensory attachments) to the universality of our super-consciousness (being reborn). It could also refer to our leaving our physical body at the time of our transition (graduation from skin school) and morphing into our spiritual body (being reborn intact and pure).)

Insperiences

Insperience is a term I coined: it means focusing on inner awarenesses like meditation, visualization, mystical visions, and introspection in contrast to experiences 'out there' which involve the five physical senses and an outer experiential focus.

By going inside to your innermost being you can know (feel, understand) the whole outside world, including the physical universe.

The rumble-and-tumbleness of the physical world, the uncertainties of the world 'out there,' the constant noise and chatter that bombard your physical senses, are not the calming influences you need to live a stress-free life. It will take the peace, calmness and serenity you gain from insperiences to center you and keep you focused on who you really are.

Intuitive Sense

Many people refer to our intuition as the sixth sense, but I call it our first sense. Why? Superior intuition is the 'Still Small Voice' of our higher Spiritual Self, our Logos Nature. It's the spiritual sense, inner voice, that activates when we quiet our five physical senses. It's the powerful 'inside voice' that tames our outside circumstances and keeps us balanced and ready to divinely order our human experiences.

ॐ   ॐ   ॐ

Jacob's Ladder

The story of Jacob's Ladder is an ancient allegorical tale that describes the alchemical process of achieving full and complete *Self-Realization* (Brahmanhood, Christhood, Buddhahood, Allahhood, Krishnahood—in short, enlightenment). It's a symbolic alchemical ladder that we all must 'climb' if we wish to reach the spiritual heights of our Divine Nature while we are embodied in physical envelops here in skin school.

As we 'climb,' we must purify ourselves—our thoughts, choices, habits and actions—so we can reach higher and higher steps in our human ascent (spiritual awakening) to consciously recover the 'Imprisoned Splendor' Robert Browning talked about in his poem, Paracelsus.

Jacob's Ladder represents the descent (a lower level of awareness) from our pre-incarnational spiritual 'embodiment' (involution from Spirit into matter) and our evolution from matter back to our etheralized spiritual nature. Each rung (level of energetic spiritual expression) represents a higher—or lower—level of cosmic awareness, adeptship and/or state of transcendent beingness.

Here are just a few snapshots of humankind's attempts through the ages to explain what Jacob's Ladder represents:

Jacob's Ladder was thought to be a 'consciousness bridge' between the earth and heaven. Interestingly, the Hebrew word for ladder, *sulam*, and the name for the mountain on which the Torah was given, Sinai, have the same *gematria* (numerical value of the letters).

According to Midrashic legend, angels who are assigned to further soul work ascend to heaven and angels assigned to incarnational work descend into the dense Earth plane to help us humans here.

Origen, an extremely accomplished 3rd Century Christian theologian, explains that there are two ladders in the life of a Christian: the ascetic ladder that the soul climbs in skin school (our earth experience) to gain enlightenment; and the soul's travel after death, climbing up the heavens (elevated states of being) towards the light of God.

Christian esotericists see Jesus figuratively as the ladder, in that his *Christ Nature* (messianic nature) bridges the gap between Heaven and Earth. Other Christian theologians describe the 'Ladder' as a seven step initiatory path to complete spiritual illumination while we are living breathing human beings.

Islamic mystics see the ladder representing the universe which stretches from heaven to earth, with angels going up and down upon it. It is the 'straight path' of creation itself which is retraced from its end back to its beginning.

Homer describes Jacob's Ladder as Jupiter's chain reaching from heaven to earth. In the Mysteries of Mithras, the ladder with its seven rounds was a symbol that referred to the ascent through the spheres of the seven planets.

In Dante's *Divine Comedy*, the eagle with golden wings that swoops down to snatch up Dante is similar to the angels descending down the ladder from heaven to earth in the story of Jacob's Ladder in the Biblical account.

As you can see the levels of interpretation of the deeper spiritual meanings associated with Jacob's Ladder are varied and in some cases riveting. From our MetaSpiritual perspective, Jacob's Ladder is an allegory that describes our chakra system. Each 'rung' symbolizes a particular spiritual energy center (chakra) from our Base Chakra to our Crown Chakra. From a molecular level, a 'twisted' Ladder could represent the Double Helix in our DNA configuration.

The seven churches in the *Book of Revelation* represent the seven major spiritual energy centers (chakras) in our body that are vital consciousness centers for our journey toward enlightenment. The seven major chakras (churches) could very well symbolize Jacob's Ladder with *each rung* representing a higher level of consciousness.

I believe the 'consciousness bridge' mentioned above is our spinal cord with heaven and earth being our super-consciousness and waking consciousness respectively. The 'angels' are the spiritually-attuned thoughts and insights that are the result of our awakening and lead to our enlightenment. (See our metaphysical interpretation of the *Book of Revelation* for a more detailed description of the kundalini's rise through our chakras).

Jacob's Pillow Stone

Jacob's pillow stone (also called the Stone of Jacob) is mentioned in the *Book of Genesis* (28:10-22) as the stone Jacob used as a pillow at the place later called Bethel (House of El, or House of God).

According to the literalist Biblical account, Jacob had fled from his twin brother Esau, whom he had tricked out of receiving their father, Isaac's, blessing which was customarily bestowed on the first-born. During his flight, Jacob rested at a city called Luz and used a couple of stones as a pillow. (If you've ever camped, you've probably done the same thing).

In a dream that night Jacob saw a ladder extending from heaven to the earth with what he thought were angels of God ascending and descending on it. He believed God told him that the land on which he slept would be given to him and his descendants.

Tradition has it that the 'pillow stone' was taken to Egypt, and later to the Promised Land when the Israelites came out of Egypt. The 'pillow stone' remained in Jerusalem until after 586 BCE when

Jerusalem was destroyed. According to legend it, along with the daughter of Zedekiah, was taken by the prophet Jeremiah to Ireland.

After this time, the kings of Ireland would be crowned while seated upon the oblong block of red sandstone called the Pillar Stone of Jacob. It was also called the Stone of Scone, the Stone of Destiny, and/or the Coronation Stone. The stone's authenticity has been surrounded with controversy throughout the centuries. The size of the stone weighing 335 pounds that is supposed to be the 'pillow stone' is about 26 inches by 16.75 inches by 10.5 inches. It was last used in 1953 for the coronation of Elizabeth II of the United Kingdom of Great Britain and Northern Ireland.

What I have just alluded to above is the checkered history of the 'stone.' Esoterically speaking, the stone on which Jacob is supposed to have rested his head has an entirely different meaning because it's an intra-cranial story of something that occurred inside Jacob's head – and subsequently within our own heads.

From a MetaSpiritual perspective, I believe the Jacob's pillow stone story is a metaphor for what can happen to all of us when we have a fully developed and disciplined use of the pituitary gland. And if there's a 'rock-hard head rest' involved, it's more than likely alluding to the fact that our pituitary gland sits in a bony hollow structure called the pituitary fossa. This bony structure is behind the bridge of the nose and below the base of our brain, close to the optic nerves. The pituitary gland is often considered the most important part of the endocrine system because it produces hormones that control many functions of other endocrine glands.

MetaSpiritually, the pituitary gland is the higher consciousness center for seership, clairvoyance, precognition, and even prophecy. When this Brow Chakra neurocenter is kept active, the energy from the Base Chakra rises up to meet the incoming energy from the Crown Chakra which we have constant access to through the pituitary gland. We can, as Jacob—and others—did, envision infinity and the inter-dimensional dynamics of the interplay between Spirit and matter. The ladder Jacob saw is more than likely our fully functioning chakra system with the seven main chakras as the rungs of the ladder.

According to ancient esoteric traditions, the pituitary gland represents the feminine principle and the pineal the masculine. When the pineal and pituitary glands are in psychic balance and operating simultaneously—as the Jacob's pillow story exemplifies —*a synchronized or quantum-equilibrium state* is created within our brain, and this synchronization allows us to connect with dimensions beyond the physical world.

So, the 'pillowed head rest' is more likely to be the fully awakened—not drowsy—interaction between the pituitary gland (protected by the boney structure called the pituitary fossa) and pineal gland which optimize each other's psychic qualities.

By the way, this interpretation is more in line with the whole story surrounding the sale of Esau's birthright to Jacob in Genesis 25: 27-34. Esau represents a lower state of awareness that is addicted to the sensory, 'touchy-feely' side of life that revolves around physical appetites and creature comforts without any thought given to spiritual aspirations.

Our quest for enlightenment means we must give up our attachments to the ego's compulsive sensory desires (red stew, pottage) which keep us in a worldly egoic consciousness (Esau) and strive to develop a higher state of consciousness (Haran) which leads us to experience the kind of spiritual visions and divine guidance that epitomize our attainment of an extremely high level of cosmic consciousness (Bethel).

Jesus' Twin

Did Yeshua (Jesus) have a twin brother? The New Testament texts we have do not support Jesus' twinship. Although, they do mention that Jesus had brothers and sisters, though the sisters aren't named. A list of brothers is recorded in Matthew 13:55, where four are mentioned: James, Joseph, Simon, and Judas. (It's unlikely that the last brother mentioned, Judas, is the one who betrayed Jesus). There is, however, a real possibility that the last brother, Judas, is Didymus Judas Thomas.

The non-canonical *Book of Thomas the Contender* suggests that Jesus had a twin brother: "Jesus said 'Now, since it has been said that you are my twin and true companion, examine yourself

…'" On this interpretation Jesus seems to have had a twin brother, also born of Mary. According to this account, one child was divine, the other an 'ordinary human being.' However, as I mentioned before, there is absolutely no evidence to support Jesus having a twin brother, although the story is not without precedent in classical mythology.

You've no doubt heard of the Greek hero Heracles (Hercules), who had a mortal twin named Iphicles. According to the myth, his parents, Alcmene and Amphitryon conceived a child. Alcmene was a beautiful woman and attracted the amorous attentions of Zeus, who made love to her in human form disguised as her husband. As a result of these couplings two infants grew in her womb, one the son of a mortal husband and wife, the other the son of a god who procreated with a mortal woman.

So, according to the story, the 'normal' impregnation (male human to female human) came first. Then there occurred the extraordinary fertilization of Alcmene with the sperm of Zeus. The product of the first impregnation was the mortal Iphicles. Hercules, whose heroic stature approached, but did not quite attain the status of a god, was reported to be the product of Alcmene's and Zeus' union.

In the case of Mary, mother of Yeshua (Jesus), the birth order is reversed. First she was impregnated by the Holy Spirit, while she was still a virgin. Then, as the story goes, not long thereafter, Joseph (or some other man) impregnated her with the child who was to become Didymus Judas Thomas, Jesus' twin brother, who was denied divine status.

Here's my take on the 'twin' of Jesus myth: At his level of enlightenment Yeshua (Jesus) could very well have bi-located, thus confusing people who saw him in one place and then heard he was seen in another place at the same time. However, I believe it's much more feasible that when his human self became consciously one with, completely aligned with, and completely *Self-Realized* with his *Cosmic Logos Nature (Higher Spiritual Self)*, 'twins' were formed. A complete oneness (twinship) was established. However, the twinship didn't involve two people—Jesus and Didymus, or anyone else. It was between Yeshua's own highly evolved humanness and his own *Higher Spiritual Nature (Cosmic Logos Nature)*. That's the 'twinship' I can buy into!

Jewish Liturgy vs. Christian Literalism

Much of the synoptic gospels, actually a good amount of their content, was written as Jewish liturgical documents, primarily for liturgical study in synagogues, as evidenced by they're being filled with plenty of Old Testament content. An orthodox Jew would tell you that the majority of what was reported was not written as historical happenings.

Many of the stories about Yeshua (Jesus) were meant to be liturgically learned and not to be taken as literal history. If the truth be told, his story is more than likely based on the liturgical year to sell Yeshua (Jesus) as the long-awaited-for messiah: Passover (Beginning of Jewish nation; Shavout (Pentecost—Jesus was the 'new' Moses; Moses gives 10 Commandments, Jesus gives the Sermon on the Mount); Rosh Hashanah (Jewish New Year); Yom Kippur (Atonement); Sukkoth (harvest festival—Jewish Thanksgiving); Hannukkah (Dedication—begins in December, festival of light (Jesus) coming into darkness (human experience); Ab (fall of Jerusalem and Temple destroyed by Babylonians; and Purim (deliverance of Jewish people from Persians). Seems pretty straightforward, doesn't it!

John the Baptizer

John the Baptizer was most likely a remastered Elijah (Malachi 3-4). He is pitched as an Elijah-like figure in the New Testament story to fulfill the Elijah role which, according to Jewish tradition, must 'come before the messiah' to announce his arrival. (See Isaiah 40:3; Malachi 3:1; 4:5). John the Baptizer was clothed in the attire of Elijah - camel's hair garments with a leather girdle at his loins - (See I Kings 1:8; Mark 1:6; Matthew 3:4). The rugged forbearer story is liturgical mythmaking. The Baptizer is clearly a remastered Elijah dressed up in New Testament clothes.

You'll need to read the Elijah, priests of Baal, and Jezebel stories in I Kings 18:20-46 to see the unmistakable connection between John the Baptizer and Elijah. The upshot is, John had to die in the New Testament story because Elijah was to be beheaded in the Old Testament account at the bequest of Jezebel, because Elijah had single-handedly beheaded 400 priests of Baal. John, as the remastered Elijah, was beheaded because the Old Testament profit wasn't! At the whim of the New Testament's 'Jezebel' (Queen Herodias), John lost his head. What I've just presented to you is liturgical conjecture concerning the relationship between two Old Testament characters and their remastered New Testament counterparts. You can draw your own conclusions.

Joseph of Nazareth

In an apocryphal gospel called the *Proto-Gospel of James*, Mary was selected at a very young age to carry the messiah. She was supposedly raised by a group of holy women who made sure she was married to an older man who would be too old to be interested in sexual intimacy in order to protect her virginity. (See how stories are concocted to retail what you want to sell). So, a man named Joseph was written into the New Testament storyline.

The New Testament Joseph was almost certainly patterned after Joseph of the 'coat of many colors' in Genesis 37-50. Both Josephs had fathers named Jacob; both are overwhelmingly identified with having life-altering dreams; and both saved the Jewish people from death (Joseph of the Old Testament saved his people from starvation. Joseph of the gospels saved his own son, Jesus, from Herod).

Joseph of the New Testament, the supposed father of Yeshua (Jesus), probably never lived as an actual New Testament character! He was most likely a literary character who was conveniently concocted to symbolize bringing the Jewish people into one united nation through the miraculous birth of the long-awaited-for messiah.

The story of Mary and Joseph taking the 12 year old Yeshua (Jesus) to Jerusalem is most probably entirely based on the Old Testament story of Samuel being taken to Shiloh. Also, Luke's John the Baptizer story appears to be based on the Genesis account of Isaac's birth (Genesis 18:9-15). Once again, read these accounts for yourself and draw your own common sense conclusions.

Judas Iscariot's Supposed Betrayal

MetaSpiritually, Judas symbolizes the self-aggrandizing aspect of our egocentric nature that seeks material means toward spiritual ends. So, was Jesus betrayed by Judas, a person of history? (The Buddhists tell a similar betrayal story where Devadatta betrayed the Buddha). I believe the betrayal story in the synoptic gospels is archetypical and not historical. (Before you betray your own illumination – and common sense - hear me out). Here's why I believe a MetaSpiritual treatment is apropos: Paul's description of the betrayal in I Corinthians 11:23-32 doesn't say anything about a betrayal by one of the apostles. Read it. See for yourself! Then you may want to read a bit further - in I Corinthians 15:4-5 – to discover that Paul states that the risen Cosmic Logos (misapplied as the Christ in the New Testament) appeared to 'the twelve' three days after Jesus' resurrection. And according to Acts 1:23, 26, it wasn't until after the ascension of Jesus that the disciples met in an upper room and chose Matthias to replace Judas as one of the 'twelve.' This suggests Judas was still alive and kicking three days after the resurrection. It also suggests that either the betrayal was a non-event or the apostles had forgiven Judas – which, although part of Jesus' teachings, probably didn't happen.

I'm not buying the historical authenticity of Judas for a number of reasons, including these, rather obvious reasons: Judas' supposed' betrayal sounds an awful lot like a compilation of Ahithophel's betrayal of King David in II Samuel 15:12 - 17:23; the 'thirty pieces of silver' reference in Zechariah 11:12; and the pretense of a 'kiss of friendship' by Joab to congratulate his cousin, Amasa in II Samuel 17:25. Read the storylines. Parts of each Old Testament story are almost identical with the New Testament betrayal story! Judas Iscariot is most likely a composite of various betrayal stories in the Hebrew Testament (Old Testament). All four stories are archetypical of our exploits, mistakes and intrigues on our spiritual journey as we unfold into our Divine Nature.

Judgment Day

'Judgment Day,' in my opinion, happens every time you make a choice or take an action (set causes into motion). If you're "punished" at all, you suffer the consequences of your own thoughts and deeds. Your thoughts and deeds are continually producing results either 'for' or 'against' your spiritual growth. No one escapes the 'Day of Judgment,' because it's taking place every day, every moment of your life. Periodic self-assessments of your spiritual, personal and professional progress are 'Judgment Days.' Every time you choose truth over error, etc., you are experiencing Judgment Day – in my 'rummaging for the truth' opinion!

ॐ   ॐ   ॐ

Know Thyself

Inscribed in the forecourt at the Temple of Apollo at Delphi is the maxim, "Know Thyself." Cher and I have modified that maxim and changed it to three words with the third word 'Self' capitalized (Know Your Self). We think this ancient maxim is talking about your capital 'S' Self (your Divine Self, your God Essence).

When you know your capital 'S' Self, your life gets easier down here in skin school.

ॐ   ॐ   ॐ

Lack Consciousness

The veil between lack and plenty and manifestation and insufficiency is the 'curtain of doubt' we manufacture to conceal our own feelings of unworthiness.

Land of Nod

The author of Genesis tells us that Cain "went out from the presence of the Lord, and dwelt in the land of Nod, east of Eden…" (Genesis. 4:16). The Hebrew word for 'Nod' means 'restless wandering, constant drifting, bewilderment, or straying.' From a literal interpretation of scripture, the Land of Nod seems to be a physical place, a geographical location. It could also symbolize a special kind of existence. From a MetaSpiritual perspective Nod isn't a place at all. It's a state of consciousness! So, before you 'nod' off, I'm going to explain my reasoning.

MetaSpiritually, 'to wander aimlessly' (the Land of Nod) implies vacillating in and out of higher thought processes by going from ordinary awareness (our Cain-ness) to super-conscious awareness (our enlightened Abel-ness) and back again into an ordinary awareness (our sleepy, drowsy or even comatose Cain nature). I believe our 'restless wandering' could also refer to our reincarnating again and again into the physical realm (skin school).

Lataif-e-Sitta

According to the Sufi tradition, *Lataif-e-Sitta* refers to the supra-sensory, psycho-spiritual 'centers' or higher consciousness faculties that are similar to the chakras. The lataif (thrill or singing) of the multicolored centers when they open signifies you're becoming enlightened. (See our Chakras reference.)

'Leave Your Nets'

MetaSpiritually, our 'nets' are fabricated out of the attachments, assumptions and emotional knots we've woven out of our limited understanding of who we are and why we're involved in another human experience. The 'call' of our *True Divine Nature* is to leave our 'nets'—to drop our dependence on the world of outer appearances—and live wholly and confidently in the knowledge that we are the flesh and blood expressions of the *One Reality* (the Eternal Presence, the Infinite Isness, God, the Universal Beingness, the Oversoul, Pure Universal Consciousness, etc.).

When you think about it, 'leaving your nets' means to stop depending on strictly material means of making a living. It means choosing to live at the speed of your enlightenment so your *Divine Nature* can guarantee your netting the 'prophet' in you in proportion to the amount of faith you have in your alignment (oneing) with your *Higher Spiritual Nature.*

Lemuric Consciousness

Lemuric consciousness means moving from one cusp of consciousness to another as we seek to acclimate ourselves to the dynamic interplay between our physical, emotional and spiritual selves on the material plane.

Lessons

Many people think we're here to learn lessons. We're not here to learn lessons. We're here to lessen Self-negating learning!

Library of Alexandria Resurrected

The ancient Library of Alexandria in Alexandria, Egypt, was one of the largest and most significant libraries in the ancient world. It was dedicated to the Muses, the nine goddesses of the arts. It flourished under the patronage of the Ptolemaic Dynasty and was the premiere center of scholarship in the 3rd century BCE until the Roman conquest of Egypt in 30 BCE. The library was destroyed four times – in 48 BCE by Julius Caesar, in 270 CE by Aurelian, in 391 CE by Coptic Pope Theophilus, and in 642 CE by Muslim general Amr ibn al'Aas who burned the library on the orders of Caliph Omar. I'd like to suggest that the worldwide Internet as a whole is a 'sorta kinda' modern day virtual Library of Alexandria, a digitized Akashic Records. Why a 'sorta kinda' version? Because the Internet contains material that is less than wholesome. Much of its content comes from the underbelly of human consciousness as well as the highest and most noble thinking.

Light Bringers

We all have a private inner realm in our mind and soul where memories of those whose names are not household names and who are not famous names in history dwell. They are there because they have made an impact on our lives. They are and have been catalysts, transforming our lives for the better. They are immortal light bringers, personal saviors, THE PEOPLE who have made a difference in our lives. They are the people to whom our personal and professional biographies are dedicated.

Liliputian Consciousness

Particles smaller than subatomic particles include, but are not limited to—quarks, hadrons (tetraquarks, fermions (baryons, hyperons), leptons (muons, taus, neutrinos), and bosons (gluons, photons, Z bosons, and W bosons). These particles are not subject, in any way shape or form, to the spacetime 'rules' many quantum physicists propose. At this level of gluonated, bosonated, muonated consciousness the charge radius of particles is known and operative, but is concealed by the fundamental masslessness of all particles smaller than subatomic particles at this level of being.

Why? Because Lilliputian Consciousness takes us into the realm of pure ethereality. Conscious awareness at this level of Pure Universal Beingness travels so fast that retro-causation (effects occurring before their causes) is commonplace.

Limitations

You can break out of any limitation, or setback, or derailment if you've upped your consciousness to a spiritual level of discernment and positivity.

The Lineage of Jesus (Yeshua)

The lineage of Yeshua (Jesus), if taken literally, is questionable. Don't take my word for it. There's plenty of credible Biblical scholars who would agree. Yeshua's lineage flows through the incest of Tamar (Genesis 38), the prostitution of Rahab (Joshua

2,6), the seduction of Ruth (Ruth1), and the adultery of Bathsheba (II Samuel 11). These stories were meant to be archetypical explanations of the evolving story of bringing light into the world. For example, MetaSpiritually, Tamar symbolizes our ability to overcome the limitations of the human experience; Rahab represents our ability to recognize and use spiritual truths and principles to keep us above the temptations of materialism; Ruth stands for our willingness to subordinate our egocentric nature to our Divine Nature; Bathsheba symbolizes our ability to energize all seven of our major chakras to ready ourselves for enlightenment.

So you see, this 'lineage' interpreted MetaSpiritually, describes our evolution in consciousness (upping our consciousness) which allows us to 'give birth' to our *Self Realization.*

Living at the Speed of the Extraordinary You

Living at the speed of the *Extraordinary You (your Higher Spiritual Nature, your I Am Nature)* doesn't mean vegging out on the sofa channel surfing. It means putting feet to your beliefs and values, putting self-improvement principles into action, constantly moving toward *Self-Realization*, and letting your Inner Strength guide you every day. So, let the *Extraordinary You* out so you can be the kind of person who can stay the course, who uses your Inner Strength to *be the best you, the most tenacious you, the most stick-to-itive you you can be!*

Logoic Seed

Through the powers of superior discernment you'll 'see' that the Cosmic Logos (Logoic Seed) underwrites the maintenance of your purified understanding; the repair of all four discordant aspects of your human encasement: emotions, physical body, etheric body, and intellect (four beasts); and the fine-tuning of your cranial nerves (elders). With your I-Am-ness expressing Itself as the Logoic Seed in human form as you, you'll be able to disentangle yourself from your small 's' self by aligning (oneing) yourself with your capital 'S' Self. That means you must not repress your Higher Spiritual Self.

Once you maintain a tight alignment (oneing) with your *Logos Nature,* you'll experience the divine power and majesty of all of the major chakras as well as benefit from their superior metaphysical essences. Harnessing the powerful energies and visionary capabilities of your chakra system will help you capture the Universal Truth Principles you need to guarantee your eventual illumination. And that illumination can be just a thought, an insight, an intuition away. It doesn't have to take as many lifetimes as you've probably been told. (See the *Cosmic Logos* reference.)

Looney Tunes

Looney Tunes are any mainstream religious assertion that diminishes, minimizes, subordinates, and debases the value, status, and importance of women, people of color, and same sex couples. They're also the silly songs we 'sing' that are composed of self-defeating, self-negating, and self-diminishing lyrics. They include the rejection by certain religious groups of medical interventions and the use of medicines that can alleviate pain and suffering. They also include fossilized religious doctrines that fail to see the truth of scientific discoveries and research findings.

Lord's Prayer

According to many Bible scholars, the Lord's Prayer was not authored by Jesus. It was a creation of the church and never taught by Jesus. Don't take my word for it. Investigate that inconvenient truth yourself.

Lotus of Being

The opening of each of our chakras marks important stages in our awakening, and each chakra is composed of petals that open when they are activated. These petals are energy structures in very fine grades of the etheric planes, and they are truly organic in their unfolding, going from a bud in the early stages of awakening, then open just like a flower, with varying numbers of petals - depending on which chakra is involved. Then they radiate gloriously in full spherical power when fully opened. The opening of the petals is not just a metaphor—the 'thrilling' (openings) are commonly observable events in the evolution of human consciousness as we move toward our eventual enlightenment.

Lotus of Control

An Internal 'Lotus of Control' describes what psychologists call our *True* or *Authentic Nature.* It's what neuroscientists refer to as our *Deeper Self.* Philosophers and spiritual teachers call it our *Higher Self* or *Divine Nature.* Cher and I call it the *Extraordinary You,* your *SuperSelf*™, your *Logos Nature*, your H*igher Spiritual Nature* for the following reasons:

One of the occupational benefits of being progressive metaphysicians and rebellious Unity ministers is that Cher and I don't hesitate dumping dogma and re-languaging traditional terms like 'Internal Locus of Control!' As you can see, Cher and I have changed the word 'locus' to 'lotus,' so that the phrase says 'Internal LOTUS of Control.' In our opinion, Cher's and my opinion, we believe the innate LOTUS POWER in you and—in everyone—will help you do what you've come here to do: walk the spiritual path on practical, loving, compassionate, enlightened, lotus-inspired feet!

Love Your Enemies

To love (harmonize, unify) your enemies (error thoughts, poor choices, divinity-denying actions) means to transform discordant thoughts, choices and actions into their higher spiritual essences. Raising your consciousness to its highest, most elevated level will help you Feng Shui your 'enemies' out of your consciousness.

ॐ   ॐ   ॐ

Mainstream Christianity

Mainstream Christianity, including religious fundamentalism, is built on the belief of human alienation from an anthropomorphic god in the sky separate from us. And this 'alienation complex' has birthed an atonement theology that reflects our supposed 'fall from grace.' I prefer an 'at-one-ment' spiritual perspective that focuses on our worthship as spiritual beings having a human experience and affirms our oneness as indivisible human extensions of the One Reality (Pure Universal Consciousness, Infinite Isness, Eternal Presence). (See the Worthship reference.)

Fear-based religions may create symptoms that mirror post-traumatic stress disorder. So, it seems that scaring and shaming people into submission by threatening 'everlasting hell, Judgment Day and punishment' are tactics that appear to be hazardous to your health. Brain-scan studies have shown that once we anticipate a future negative event, activity in the amygdala is turned up and activity in the anterior cingulate is turned down.

Mainstream Christianity has no answer for the restless searchings of the human heart which seeks a deeper and more meaningful understanding of our relationship with God (the One Reality, Pure Universal Consciousness) and the universe. How can an imploding theology lead people anywhere, since it fails to see that the Cosmic Logos underwrites the True Nature of everything.

Manacled Miniaturization

The price you pay for mindless conformity to religious dogma and literal-only interpretations of sacred scripture is being manacled to religious staleness which minimizes your spiritual growth. Staying 'unmanacled' means attending spiritual retreats and conferences; finding top-notch TV, YouTubes, and websites on spirituality; cultivating your own meditational and/or affirmative prayer practice; forming study groups with like-minded people; leaving dogma completely behind; engaging in your own 'heavy' reading, writing, and blogging; and traveling to spiritual sites all around the world. It means freeing your hands for service and opening your mind up to metaphysical and esoteric thought; disciplined meditation; and getting to know more about sciences such as neuroscience, evolutionary biology, optogenetics and quantum physics. Take the manacles off and free yourself from the limitations of stale religious programming and fossilized beliefs that keep you handcuffed and out of the 'enlightenment loop.'

The **Manger**

The *Cosmic Logos* is 'borne' in the manger of human consciousness and expresses Itself more and more as we become more Self-Realized, knowing that our beingness is the One Reality's Beingness actualized in human form as us.

The **Mark of Cain**

You may have heard of the Bible story of Cain and Abel. It's a well-known tale about brothers who may or may not have been twins since some accounts have Cain being born many years before Abel. Nevertheless, it's quite a story and its deeper spiritual meaning goes well beyond its literal interpretation.

According to the literalist Biblical account in Genesis, Chapter 4, which describes Cain killing his twin brother Abel, Cain says to Jehovah, "My sin is greater than I can bear! See, you have driven me out today from the face of the ground, and I will be hidden from your face. And I will be a fugitive and a wanderer on the land, and anyone who finds me will kill me."

And Jehovah said to him (apparently addressing others nearby), "Therefore whoever kills Cain will suffer a sevenfold vengeance." And Jehovah put a mark on Cain so that anyone who found him would not kill him. And Cain went out from the presence of Jehovah and lived in the land of Nod.

The word translated as 'mark' in Genesis 4:15 is '*owth*,' which means a sign, an omen, a warning, or a remembrance. Some interpretations view this 'mark' as a physical mark like a Hebrew letter, or a horn growing out of Cain's head, or a tattoo, or even a stone covering the Third Eye. Others see the 'mark, imprint or protrusion' as a sign or stigma, and not necessarily a physical mark on Cain himself. Some traditions describe the 'mark' as depriving Cain and his lineage of facial hair, which would have been very obvious since men in that time period would have been bearded.

In the Hindu epic Mahabhārata, which predates the Cain and Able story, an avatar named Ashwatthama was considered to be chief among the rishis in Kaliyuga (the last of the four stages the world goes through as part of the *cycle of yugas,* according to

Hindu scripture). Ashwatthama was born with a gem in his forehead which gave him power over all living beings lower than humans. This gem protected him from hunger, thirst, fatigue and all of the typical physical ailments.

That being said, there is, and continues to be, no clear consensus as to what Cain's 'mark' was from a literal-only perspective. However, from a MetaSpiritual perspective which considers people, places, events and things in the outer world as metaphors for what goes on inside of us, Cain's mark has a different and more compelling meaning.

In order to understand Cain at a deeper spiritual level we must understand where Cain came from, you know, who his parents were and what they symbolized spiritually. The following perspective of Cain's parents, Adam and Eve, comes from our MetaSpiritual interpretation of the Cain and Abel story which is a separate post on our website:

MetaSpiritually speaking, Adam symbolizes the archetypical movement in mind that epitomizes the reasoning, reductionist, objective, logical, deductive, methodical and judgmental nature of our pre-incarnational make-up. Adamic energies underwrite our left hemispheric brain-ness and are very much tied to our thoughts when we incarnate into human form.

Eve represents the archetypical pattern in our heart-centered awareness that epitomizes the nurturing, highly intuitive, wisdom-centered, subjective, unconditional love-oriented, social and emotive nature of our pre-incarnational make-up. Eve energies underwrite our right hemispheric brain-ness and are connected very psychically to our feelings when we incarnate into human form.

The archetypical mythical couple Adam and Eve show us that if the polarities between the head and the heart and left hemisphere and right hemisphere do not fully resonate, the products of their union (Cain and Abel, Romulus and Remus, and all of the mythical brother stories throughout history) will exhibit the disequilibrium and conflict that characterize the original pre-incarnational disconnect.

When our Cain-ness intentionally represses (kills) its inclination to honor our spiritual impulses (our Abel-ness) by expressing its attachment to the physical realm we call skin school, we are 'protected' from the stigma of rejecting our spiritual identity by forgetting we are divine beings.' I believe it is this forgetfulness (retrograde amnesia) that is the 'mark' of Cain! It protects us, incubates us, from the guilt of choosing repeated physical embodiments that mindlessly reinforce our beliefs in separation and duality.

What's more, our retrograde amnesia (the mark of Cain) causes us to inhabit a physical body which favors our egocentric consciousness over our super-consciousness. So, whoever forgets (kills) that the tendency of our left-brainedness (our Cain-ness) is to repress (kill) our spiritual impulses will suffer skin school consequences. That is, we must struggle (suffer) to regain our spiritual identity by reawakening our seven major spiritual energy centers (chakras) through disciplined and arduous soul work (a sevenfold vengeance) during each incarnation.

For most of us our entire skin school experience involves re-establishing the alignment between our hemispheric Cain-ness and its 'fraternal twin hemisphere' (our Abel-ness) in order for us to transcend our worldly attachments.

Ours is an interesting sojourn in materiality, because our ego is always in a constant struggle to kill off our higher, more spiritual nature. Our ego wants total control, because to sacrifice its temporal rulership is to die to our worldly self and let our Divine Nature live through, in and as us! And for most of us that's something the ego is unwilling to do. You notice I said most of us – there are those enlightened beings who are subordinating their egos to their higher spiritual nature everyday. It means enabling your Abel-ness and canning your Cain-ness – in my opinion! (See our *Where Did Cain Get His Wife?* blog article on our website: TheGlobalCenterForSpiritualAwakening.com)

Maskunfusion

When you let your innate divinity light radiate, you turn mass-confusion into mask-unfusion … unfusing the many masks you have chosen to put on, which have dimmed your light, and created an illusion of separation from the Truth of who you really are. When you allow yourself to wear a mask too long, it begins to become a part of you, and you start to believe it's who you really are. The mask can stick to you like glue unless you unmask yourself.

Sometimes our masks wear masks! For example, a mask of lack consciousness can wear a mask of being conservative and economical with our money. Now there is absolutely nothing wrong with being conservative and economical — unless it's grounded in a fear of not having enough. You know when you have a mask on, because it's extremely uncomfortable. If you're feeling out of sync, unhappy, frustrated, scared, angry, or having any feeling that's not a feeling of at-one-ment with your *Higher Spiritual Nature*, you know you're wearing one of these negatively-charged masks.

Meditation

According to neuroscientist T.J. Davidson and psychologist Dan Goleman, who shared research related to a psychological perspective on transformations of consciousness, you can literally change your brain's neural circuitry in important and life-affirming ways by engaging in meditation every day for only an hour each day.

Meditation has no built-in limitations. There are only limiting thoughts about it.

Meditation is being consciously one with your Cosmic Beingness. When you meditate you raise the spiritual octave of humankind's collective consciousness in direct proportion to your own depth of inner being.

Meditate now or loose traction toward your Self-Realization.

Meditation is not only constant Self-awareness of your capital 'S' Self (your Divine Nature), but constant abandonment of the small 's' self (your egocentric nature).

> *People who object to meditation are*
> *trivializing their enlightenment.*

Meditation is not the means to an end! And to say that it is both the means and the end is misleading, too, because when you are in a meditative state, you are in a non-local universe of super-conscious thought. You achieve conscious oneness with the One Reality that is the Ground of All Being and Non-being. There is no beginning or end because there are no parameters in Pure Universal Consciousness as far as we know. At your super-conscious level, you are in a higher consciousness realm where everything IS INSTANTANEOUS. There is no such thing called spacetime, because that would imply distance, and in the realm of the Absolute (the One Reality) there is no need to move toward anything. *YOU ARE EVERYTHING, EVERYWHERE ALL AT ONCE!*

Your **Mental Portal**

When you truly seek to live a Cosmic Logos-centric life, nothing (no thing) can enter your consciousness to defile you without your consent. Your conscious alignment (oneing) with the truth of who you really are constantly stands guard at your mental portal to admit only what is real and harmonious with your elevated level of awareness.

Metaphysical Study

The term 'metaphysical' does not need to have enigmatic mystical, esoteric or magical overtones – and certainly no taint of woo-woo-ness. That which is metaphysical is simply a level of heightened awareness that sees people, places, things and events beyond their physical face value and far above their literalness.

I can resist everything except my beautiful wife and a metaphysical interpretation of Biblical scripture.

You can be very metaphysical and mystical, but you will still need to know the passwords to your iphone, online bank account, app store, MicroSoft updates, etc.

When you experience the awesome depth of metaphysical *Bible, Torah* and *Qur'an* interpretations and the insights you gain from their esoteric bandwidths, you will feel their unmissableness as they relate to your spiritual growth.

I've found that being an outspoken metaphysician and rebellious Unity minister may not inspire some people to give up a literal interpretation of scripture, but it may annoy enough people to prompt them to challenge unquestioned answers.

Metaphysical study is a form of recess. You take a recess from dogma, a literalization of scripture, and patriarchal storytelling.

Metaphysicians share their knowledge because they have something to say; dogmatists proselytize because they have to say something that retails their close-mindedness.

MetaSpirituality

MetaSpirituality is 'now moment ontology' and '21st century metaphysics' morphed into a timeless perspective.

MetaSpirituality isn't about thinking something up. It's just the opposite—it's bringing rarified spiritual principles down to earth.

MetaSpirituality generally interferes with dogmatic biases, denominational sparring, religious exclusivity, mainstream churches' science phobia, and the denigration of women and same sex couples. One of the things Cher and I love about MetaSpiritual conversations is their endless bandwidth of perspectives. And that's good, because too much agreement and conformity kill a good chat.

One of MetaSpirituality's purposes is to replace a dogmatic mindset with an open one.

Migration Patterns

Migration patterns are spiritual thoughts, words and actions that migrate into worldly thoughts, words and actions, and vice versa. The intensity and frequency of each respective pattern shows if you are more spiritually directed or materially inclined.

Mind Auction or Mind Action

We have many thoughts during the course of a day. Some thoughts 'drive by' like the vehicles we see on highways. Others linger or even repeat themselves. The important thing you need to know about thoughts is that your thoughts determine your inclinations, your inclinations lead to choices, and your choices lead to actions.

Thoughts and emotions don't happen in a vacuum. You choose them! They are internal reactions to an outside stimulus. You choose to get angry or irritated or impatient. When you are fearful, you choose to be fearful. If you are envious, you choose to be envious. If you are joyful, you choose to be joyful.

The thing about thinking is every thought you have either honors your authentegrity or multiplies illusion. 'Thoughts held in mind produce after their kind' is a commonly-used expression by many New Thought people. The question is, however: Thoughts produce *what* after their kind? The answer seems obvious, but I'm going to say it anyway: They produce similar thoughts. That is, they lead to thoughts which are characteristic of the consciousness which spawned them in the first place. That means that similar thoughts repeated often enough reinforce truth or perpetuate error.

That's how thoughts travel through your mind and that's how thoughts are "auctioned" too! When you control your thinking you control your thoughts. If you auction your thinking to the world of outer appearances you auction your life to the world of wishcraft, quick fixes, and 'too good to be true' schemes.

In a remarkable scientific breakthrough, researchers at Berlin's Bernstein Center for Computational Neuroscience were the first to measure intentions we hold in our mind *before* the intentions are put into action. For example, when new information enters our brains, they say, it enters into our short-term memory field. The process is called *synaptic transmission.* The electro-chemical impulses ignite one neuron, which in turn ignites another neuron.

The new information is remembered only if the second neuron repeats the impulse back again to the first. This most likely happens when we decide that the new information is important. Affirmations are a perfect example of this repeat firing process.

If the neural 'echo' is sustained long enough it amps up the brain's incredible neuroplasticity, which leads to lasting structural changes. This 'echo' hard wires the new information, forming memory grooves in your gray matter. That's why it's so important to think positive thoughts, watch positive TV shows and Internet programs, and play nonviolent games.

If you hard-wire your thoughts only on what you see through the filters of your five senses, you may create grooves of materiality in your consciousness which make it harder for you to see lasting happiness and success. You'll stop being robbed of your potential successes, which are all around you, when you get really good at doing three things: affirming your incredible, extraordinary awesomeness; forgiving anyone you believe may have injured or harmed you in any way; and expressing your Higher Spiritual Nature every chance you get.

When you do those three things you'll turn unwanted *mind auction* into positive *mind action.* It's so important to recognize when you are auctioning your thinking! And this self-defeating auctioning process is easy to see because the symptoms of mind auction are:

- allowing your schedule to rob you of your inner focus time … and end up never having time to do it.
- affirming you are a positive person, and then having hour-long discussions with friends about how horrible the economy is, or how helpless you are, or how unworthy you are, etc.!
- slipping into old habits of doubt, fear, or just plain give-up-ness.
- reliving hurts caused by someone close to you, and wanting to wear 'staying hurt' as a badge of honor.
- allowing excuses to take the place of healthy life styles.

- sitting back, hoping things will improve, but feeling stuck like a hamster in a cage, running in circles on the wheel!
- thinking this mind action stuff doesn't work—just because you haven't gotten the results you want.
- compromising your authentegrity by neglecting to align yourself with your Higher Spiritual Nature.

Moving from *Mind Auction* to *Mind Action* takes diligent awareness and a personal commitment to standing in the truth of who you are and practicing the Truth principles you know! It means paying attention to all thoughts that are floating in and out of your consciousness, and stop auctioning off the better parts of you!

Mindfulness

When is the last time you sat quietly for the purpose of sitting quietly? Try this: Find a quiet place, one that will allow you a few minutes of uninterrupted seclusion. Sit with your attention focused on not focusing on anything in particular. Do not attempt to concentrate on anything. When you hear something, noises that are close as well as those that are some distance away, you are listening to the immediate sounds in your current environment. Become aware that your attention is not confined to one narrow channel in particular. Listen without strain or judgment.

Find a sound and focus on it. Then focus on another sound, and then another. Now focus totally on your breathing. Sense each inhalation and exhalation. Hear the inhalations on the exhalations through your parted lips. Concentrate on your breathing for the next several minutes.

Now, repeat the 'Om' sound with each exhalation for the next few minutes. That universal sound is a prelude for hearing the alignment (oneing) you have established with your *Core Spiritual Being*. Listen for the 'Still Small Voice' in the Silence which follows. Be mindful of your own universality.

Taking things for granted is the epitome of the superficialization of life.

Mindless Endorsements

The fanatical literalist interpretation of Biblical scripture fosters the mindless endorsement of a dogmatic religious brainwashing that literally hypnotizes the 'faithful' into believing in the inerrancy of the written word. The fact that the Biblical writers—whoever they really were—either misremembered, purposefully changed, and/or invented stories about the people and events—including those about Yeshua (Jesus)—aren't usually addressed or even admitted by blurry-eyed literalists who fail to question the accuracy and historicity of Biblical texts. (See the How 'Yeshua' Became 'Jesus' and Questionable Biblical Memories references)

Molecular Consciousness

The molecular expression of Pure Beingness reminds us that molecules and atoms never die. What 'dies' is matter's coherence and physical appearance. And as a coherent collection of atoms, we are repositories of mental real estate that engineers the behavior of nerve cells, glial cells, and the atoms, ions, and molecules that make up our physical appearance.

One of the keynotes of the molecular level of understanding is that each atom of the universe is intrinsically linked with all other atoms—at every level of manifestation—through their memories and the information they carry. The mystery of how this information exchange occurs—whether through molecular structure, chemical reactions, entangled states, or some other method is understood by the 'molecular citizens' at this level.

Molecular consciousness also knows 'why and how' the information that keeps us humans alive and well—and unique—is stored in the wave packets of our molecules. The molecular level of consciousness knows that a large variety of biological molecules come from complex stellar forces and coalesce in the earth leaving ample supplies of molecules of every kind. This 'cosmic dust' includes aromatic and aliphatic type chemicals, and polycyclic aromatic hydrocarbons.

At the molecular level of conscious awareness molecules and cells seem to understand that a combination of top down causal organization and bottom up chemical evolution appear to be necessary conditions for life at all levels of complexity.

^(The) Molecular You

Inside of your body, in the microcosm of your inner being, are the subtle vibrations of a molecular world. You're composed of communes, colonies, cities and continents of trillions of cells in action. Your body is filled with cellular life. You're composed of hydrogen atoms and subatomic particles like quarks, leptons, and gluons that were present at the 'big bang' that birthed our universe. Quantum physicists tell us that we're literally stardust as physical beings. Subatomic parts of you are 13.8 billion years old. Other parts of you are a billionth of a second old. At a molecular and cellular level you're a universe that's designed as a physical container that houses your particular level of consciousness and spirituality.

You'll see that to simply describe your network of cells as only biological containers comprised of a nucleus, membrane, receptors, tubes, fluid, and genetic markers is to miss the point of your biological footprint. You'll discover that your cells are highly intelligent beings with an innate divinity all their own. Written into the biography of your cells are the mysteries of life and consciousness, involution and evolution, time and space, the universe and the Multiverse! Your cells are literally tabernacles of Spirit.

Molehill Management

Without an awareness of your True Divine Nature much of your time is spent keeping chaos at bay, protecting your life and property, staving off financial disaster, climbing longer and longer corporate ladders, and managing the conflicts and disappointments that invariably find you. Wave against wave crashes against you. You may turn molehills into mountains, and create avalanches of fear and doubt that bury you. You may mistake assumptions as facts and half-truths as gospel. No wonder you can get confused. And once you're confused by molehills, you usually run into mountains of doubt and valleys of discontentment.

Blissful ignorance keeps us in a la-la land of false security until we have the wherewithal to come to our senses. The reason there aren't more happy people is that we have turned what could be blissful moments into blistering instances of false assumptions, unnecessary fears, and troublesome doubts. Happiness is an inside-out process. It is usually underwritten with a well-defined sense of appreciation for the conscious presence of our *Higher Spiritual Self*. Molehill management means keeping molehills *molehills*.

Mortal Coil

The length of our life is metaphorically a length of thread that is coiled on a spool, an analogy related to the ancient Greek mythological figures of the Fates. It was popularized by the "To be, or not to be," the "slings and arrows of outrageous fortune," and "to sleep, perchance to dream" soliloquies in Shakespeare's *Hamlet*. It was coined repeatedly to address the troubles and burdens life tosses at us. At various times people have used it as a verb to mean 'to cull', 'to thrash,' 'to lay in rings or spirals.' As we live, our 'mortality thread' is unwound from the coil by the shuttle of the loom of time and circumstance. So, the mortal coil refers to our tumults and troubles, our challenges and turmoils, and the trials and tribulations we face as spiritual beings having a human experience.

Mudras

What if mudras are a form of nonlocal mental shiatsu that connects your hand gestures with your soul?

Multiple Universes

At the heart of MetaSpirituality is a cosmology which holds that there are multiple world systems. At the heart of quantum physics is the theory of multiple universes springing from the Multiverse. What if the conditions for the creation of a particular universe involve "ushering" it into existence like the 'chosen sperm' is ushered and protected by the millions of other sperm in human reproduction to unite with the egg. So, the job of millions and billions of universes is to "usher in" the one universe that is primed for living beings such as ourselves.

ॐ   ॐ   ॐ

Naming God

To name the Eternal Presence (Pure Universal Consciousness, One Reality, God, The All, Infinite Isness, The Absolute, Divine Mind, and the 72, 000 other names humankind has concocted to describe the Unnameable) is to limit your awareness of the Eternal Presence. Naming the God of your understanding does not limit that God—only your conception and understanding of that God.

Nasma Body

According to Sufi philosophy, our Nasma Body is Your Vital Body (*Linga Sharira*). It's an ethereal body of the purest form of light connected to you by the silver cord (crystal cord). Without it, your physical body would not exist. (See the detailed Silver Cord reference in our book entitled *More Straight Talk About Spiritual Stuff.*)

Nativity Star

The light from stars takes millions of years to get to Earth. The light from the star that was supposed to announce Jesus' birth would have had to have been 'hung' millions of years in advance to arrive just at the right time to guide the magi. "To literalize that star in the eastern sky," says John Shelby Spong, "is to participate in astrophysical non-sense. There never was a star in the east."

The Nativity Story (Cher's and My Short Version)

How many times have you misplaced your eyeglasses or your keys or iphone or wallet or purse and looked around all over the place for them only to find them somewhere on your person? You had them all the time! And, if you're like Cher and me, you probably felt a little foolish searching for something 'out there' that you didn't have to search for at all!

I've just described the short version of the Nativity story! You don't have to look 'out there' for a messiah or savior or higher spiritual being. It's not 'out there.' You don't have to wait. Your connection to the One Reality is 'in here.'(We're pointing to our head and heart). It's your *Higher Spiritual Self*, your *Logos Nature*.

Nirvana

Since my wife, Cher, and I have an online ministry called The Global Center for Spiritual Awakening, much of our work has to do with the concept of Nirvana. We spend a lot of time on our computers, adding new content (blogs, articles, Facebook and YouTube posts, product sales sheets, etc.). It just occurred to me that Cher, who is our Internet guru, may have achieved *Nerd-vana*.

Noah's Ark

The concept of an 'ark' has been floating around in the stream of human thought for thousands of years (excuse the pun). Depending on the spiritual depths you want to plummet in getting a sense of the esoteric dimensions of 'your arkness,' you are free to explore this subject to your heart's content. A few of the most well-known flood motifs are: the Mesopotamian flood stories (Atrahasis; Gilgamesh; and Ziusudra, the Sumerian Noah), the Deucalion in Greek mythology where the 'ark' finally landed on Mt. Parnassus, the Hindu avatar Vishnu warning Manu of an impending flood in the Satapatha Brahmana, the Mayan flood story, the Muisca Bocchica of South American deluge, the Lac Courte Oreilles Ojibwa Native American flood myth, the Gun-Yu flood myth of China, the Finnish flood myth in the Kalevala rune, the Australian Tiddalik deluge, and the Polynesian Nu'u flood.

Cher and I believe all of the 'ark' and flood stories in sacred literature are apocryphal tellings and retellings of what goes on within our own consciousness. The people and places in those stories - regardless of the culture in which they originate - represent qualities, characteristics, habits, thoughts and feelings within us.

Noah's ark can represent many 'containerized' things: your consciousness (waking conscious, subconscious and super-conscious) in and between incarnations and reincarnations; your physical body with the super-conscious as the upper 'window;' the legendary Holy Grail; the Philosopher's Stone; the Earth; the Milky Way Galaxy (our cosmic womb); our universe (one of billions); the Multiverse (one of billions that spawns billions of universes); your Quantum Self; the Field of Infinite Potential; the mythical Garden of Eden; etc. (See our Spiritually Speaking Glossary for more information on this incredible concept and related concepts.)

Nothingness

No-thing-ness is, according to MetaSpirituality, quantum physics and mysticism, a misnomer. The concept of 'nothingness' implies a void, vacuum, nonexistence or the absence of things, and may not be an accurate description of reality. Philosophically, Parmenides suggested that there can be no such things as *coming-into-being, passing-out-of-being,* or *not-being.* Aristotle postulated that space is not 'nothingness' but, rather, a receptacle in which objects of matter can be placed. Isaac Newton asserted the existence of absolute space, but for Descartes there was matter, and there was the extension of matter which left no room for the existence of 'nothingness.' For quantum physicists there's dark matter and dark energy that permeate almost all of space, and in quantum field theory, even in a vacuum there's a buzz of virtual particles that hop in and out of 'existence,' making even so called vacuum states a zero point field (a state of fleeting electromagnetic waves) filled with quantum activity. So, creating 'something from nothing' has never been true. There has always been that 'Somethingness' called Pure Universal Consciousness (One Reality, God, Logos, Brahman, Dharma, Bahá'i, Absolute, Great Spirit, The Ground of All Being, Infinite Isness, etc.) from which all things emanate and have their being.

Now Moments

We get so caught up in getting somewhere, that we often forget to just 'BE.' Throughout your day, I encourage you to just stop, take a breath, and look around you. Enjoy the journey, and embrace the wonderful surprises you encounter when you are present to the now moment. And in each moment, remind yourself to focus and be joyful, peaceful, aware. You have the power to make the choice of how to BE in every moment.

The eternal you is part of the nowness I refer to as a 'now moment.' The transcendental you is here now. The cosmic you is eternally present tense. You are your incredible potential realized in this now moment. Each moment-of-now you have an opportunity to express your wholeness simply by allowing it to surface. You don't have to go anywhere for it to unfold.

ॐ ॐ ॐ

OM 101

OM (AUM) is the primordial sound of the universe, according to Hinduism. Many people have heard that OM is about the sacred threes. However, it's really about the sacred fours. I'll explain below. OM is actually made up of three syllables: A, U, M – or phonetically (aaah, oooh and mmmm). The syllables represent trinities like: the Hindu gods (Brahma, Vishnu and Shiva); Arche, Spanda and Apeiron; the One Reality, Cosmic Logos and Holy Spirit; the Three Bodies of Buddhahood; the three emanations of Ein Sof (All That Is, Wisdom and Understanding); God, Christ and the Holy Spirit; super-consciousness, waking consciousness and subconscious; spirituality, metaphysics and science; etc.

Here's how Cher and I vocalize the OM (AUM) sound using its four vibrations to ground ourselves with the One Reality:

ॐ For 'aaah, relax your jaw. Part your lips, and make sure your tongue doesn't touch the palate. You'll notice the 'aaah' sound rises from your belly.

ॐ In 'oooh,' your lips gently come together as the sound moves from your abdomen into your heart center.

ॐ During 'mmm,' allow your tongue to float to the roof (cathedral) of your mouth, and your lips to come together to create a gentle buzzing in your head.

ॐ When your vocalization stops, sit silently for a moment. Allow silence (OM's 'fourth syllable') to complete your vocalizations. It's the silence (the quantum vacuum) that allows you to settle into the bliss of your oneness with the One Reality, Pure Universal Consciousness.

Repeat this recitation at least three times, or more, depending on your time and schedule. Your alignment with your *Divine Nature,* the purring of your soul's yearning for oneness, is the inaudible 'sound of silence' (the oneing) of your human personality with your *Higher Spiritual Self.*

Omnism

Omnism is the belief that all religions contain universal truths, but that no one religion has a copyright on all that is true. It espouses the legitimacy of differing spiritual and religious understandings of reality. Omnists are open-minded and are not prone to have or accept dogmatic religious perspectives. Omnists believe we have come too far in our studies of the social sciences, history, psychology, neuroscience, biology, culture, etc., to ignore research-based facts or take things merely on the assumption of scriptural accuracy or inerrancy. In some respects omnism is similar to MetaSpirituality in the scope of its open-mindedness.

*Your OM (AUM) Nature is your Cosmic Logos Nature
(your I Am Nature, your Higher Spiritual Self,
your Self-Realized Nature).*

OM Oomph

OM (AUM) is a sacred sound (mantra) of great importance in many Eastern religions. OM (AUM) represents the primordial abstract, absolute space that is beyond attributes or forms, yet is the origin of everything. Thus Om mystically embodies the essence of the entire universe. So, I invite you, as a spiritual practice, to start your mantras, prayers and meditations with OM. Why? Because it means that uttering the very syllable OM (AUM) guarantees results when you elevate your consciousness to an octave that connects with the Field of Infinite Potential. The sound (vibration) of your thoughts is the amperage (oomph) you will need to manifest what you want from the unmanifest. Cher and I've seen it work – that's why we recommend it. (See Undiscovered Consciousness reference).

Omvana/Omville

OM is a sacred sound (mantra) of great importance in many Eastern religions. OM represents the primordial abstract, absolute space that is beyond attributes or forms, yet is the origin of everything. Thus Om mystically embodies the essence of the entire universe.

The word Aum consists of three sounds: *a (a-kāra), u (u-kāra), and m (ma-kāra)*. *A-kara* means 'form or shape' like the earth, trees, or any other object. *U-kāra* means 'formless or shapeless' like water, air or fire. *Ma-kāra* means 'neither shape nor shapeless (but still exists)' like dark matter in the Universe.

The syllable 'Om' describes the All-Encompassing Mystical Consciousness (Pure Universal Consciousness) that started creation with an original vibration (*Cosmic Logos*) manifesting as the sound 'OM.' It is the manifestation of God (the Eternal Presence, Pure Universal Consciousness, etc.) as the *Cosmic Logos* in physicality. It is believed to be the basic sound of the world and to contain all other sounds.

Esoterically, AUM is the bow, the arrow is the Self, and Brahman (the Absolute Reality) is said to be the mark. You might find this interesting about the threefold nature of the OM symbol: OM or AUM consists of three curves, one semicircle, and a dot:

ॐ The large lower curve symbolizes our waking state which is influenced by the five physical senses.

ॐ The upper curve denotes the state of deep sleep of our subconsciousness.

ॐ The middle curve symbolizes our dream state.

ॐ The semi circle symbolizes the illusion of maya and separates the dot from the other three curves. Maya prevents us from the realization of our highest state of bliss. The semi circle is open at the top, and doesn't touch the dot. This means that this highest state is not affected by maya which only affects the manifested universe.

ॐ The dot signifies a blissful state of consciousness and is the ultimate aim of all spiritual growth.

There's a nuance about using OM that I'd like to mention again. It's the sacred fourth dimensional 'sound of silence' that follows uttering OM. It represents the omnipresence of oneness and universality that epitomizes the very nature of the universe. It reminds us that each of us is particularizations of that universal oneness and unity (Pure Universal Consciousness). We are not separate from it.

The Upanishads say that OM is Brahman in the form of sound. I agree. And I would add that we humans are the Eternal Presence (Pure Universal Consciousness as the *Cosmic Logos)* in the form of us. So, I invite you to use OM as the first word you say in your affirmations, prayers, mantras, and meditations. The OM sound will connect you to the 'Field of Infinite Potential' which will guarantee the results you want by right of consciousness … as you walk the spiritual path on practical feet!

Repeating the *'Oṃ maṇi padme hūṃ'* as a spiritual practice is a well-known six-syllabled Sanskrit mantra. Mani means 'jewel' or 'bead' and Padma means 'lotus flower, which is the Buddhist sacred flower. Cher's and my favorite translation is: *Om* purifies bliss and pride (realm of the Absolute); *Ma* purifies jealousy and the need for self-aggrandizing entertainment (realm of the jealous gods); *Ni* purifies desire for materialistic addictions (realm of human wants); *Pad* purifies ignorance and prejudice (realm of animal instincts); *Me* purifies selfishness and possessiveness (realm of the hungry ghosts); *Hum* purifies aggression and hatred (realm of a hellish state of consciousness).

Open-Mindedness

Only an inquisitive, open mind can close the door that leads to dogma and stale tradition.

Otherizing

We humans have done a good job of 'otherizing' ourselves every time we diss our *Higher Spiritual Nature* by giving into our ego's arrogance, impatience, bling whims and recurrent paranoia.

ॐ   ॐ   ॐ

Palliative Healthcare

There's a growing emphasis on quality in palliative healthcare and an increasing body of robust research demonstrating the positive impact of spiritual care, including overall patient comfort and better patient quality of life near death. More and more people want spiritual support than actually receive it, especially during times when it can make a pivotal difference - during an illness, at the end of life, and grieving the loss of a loved one.

Paper Pope

Just as the Roman Catholic Church has a pope invested with infallible religious authority for the believers, so mainstream Christian churches see the Bible as their paper pope.

Parallel Universes

I do not doubt that there are intelligent beings in adjacent dimensions and parallel universes that transcend our limited perspectives as much, or more, as we transcend a mosquito's. And, by analogy, several parallel universes are closer than we think: our egocentric consciousness, our subconsciousness, our waking consciousness, and our super-consciousness.

Parentage

It's important to strive to fill your consciousness with Divine Ideas, because the ideas which follow will manifest goodness, selflessness and altruism as the offspring of the fires of their divine parentage.

Paschal Lamb

If you give yourself a chance and rise above the embedded theology of your youth, I believe you'll see that the paschal lamb is an archetype of humankind's ability to conquer death when we 'up our consciousness' to a super-consciousness level of divine perfection. Our physical body is the cross we bear. It's the doorway to and from the world of Spirit. You no doubt recall the Passover story in the Old Testament book of Exodus (Exodus 12) where the blood of the sacrificial lamb of God was painted on the exterior doorframes of Jewish homes so they would be protected from death. What's interesting is, in the New Testament, the cross came to symbolize the 'doorpost of the world.' When Yeshua (Jesus) was crucified on the cross (the doorpost of the world) he became the new 'paschal lamb' whose spilled blood (Spiritual Life Force) proved to humankind that we can transfuse our 'blood' back to its cosmic dimension by leaving our physical body behind and returning to our more transcendent beingness without loss of consciousness and without the loss of our God essence.

The sacrificial lamb is an age old story, one that's been repeated in various degrees ever since human beings have inhabited the planet. Yeshua (Jesus) came to realize he was the *Cosmic Logos* expressing Itself as him in human form. (It's an enlightened realization we all must come to know about ourselves).

Yeshua perfectly understood his Divine Nature, fully demonstrated his innate divine potential, and completely aligned his human self with his Divine Nature (*Higher Spiritual Self*). He became fully Self-Realized. So, the paschal lamb is our Divine Nature which is housed in our flesh-and-blood physical body. Each time we incarnate we are sacrificing (incarcerating) our Divine Nature by subjugating It into a human-like form (intelligent being) in this earth dimension – or in another dimension we have chosen instead of the earth dimension. Each time we do this, assuming we have woken up and realized what a highly evolved spiritual being we really are, we get to show ourselves that we can overcome death (the illusion of separation) by becoming consciously one with our *SuperSelf*™, our *Extraordinary Divine Nature.*

Peace

Peace is the space between two thoughts.

Perfected Beings

When we become fully Self-Realized, we join Perfected Beings who have mastered their reincarnational and incarnational experiences (sojourns). This august assembly of Perfected Beings is also known as the Adept Hierarchy, World Saviors, the Mahatmas, the Seven Richis and their Successors in Hindu religious teachings, the Sangha in Buddhist teachings, the Great White Brotherhood and the Ascended Masters of Theosophy, the Priests of the Order of Melchizedek in Abrahamic religion, the Masters of Wisdom, and as Self-Realized Beings according to MetaSpirituality.

Philosopher's Stone

The *lapis philosophorum* (Philosophers' Stone) which means 'the love of truth,' is a legendary substance, supposedly capable of turning corruptible base metals into incorruptible gold. It's generally believed to be a 'substance' you can touch and hold. It's billed as the Elixir of Life, Fountain of Youth, Ambrosia, Soma, Amrita, Nectar of Immortality, responsible for rejuvenation, heavenly bliss, enlightenment, and even immortality. Some believe the Philosophers' Stone is similar to mercury or quicksilver – that is, neither solid metal nor a liquid but having both qualities – a sort of universal, ethereal quintessence (the fluid of heaven). Seen as the conjunction of polarities, the Philosophers' Stone is believed to represent the fusion of Spirit and matter.

This mythical stone has been attributed with many mystical and magical properties. Its most commonly mentioned properties are its ability to transmute base metals into gold or silver, its ability to heal all forms of illness and dis-ease, and its uncanny ability to prolong the life of anyone who samples even a small part of the Philosophers' Stone. Other mythical properties include: awakening our chakras, morphing common crystals into precious stones, reviving dead plants, and creating flexible or malleable glass objects.

For close to 1,000 years, it has been the most sought-after prize in Western alchemy. The origins of the Philosophers' Stone seem to be in ancient Hinduism. The Hindu *Yoga Vasistha*, written between the 6th or 7th and edited as late as the14th centuries CE, contains a story about the Philosophers' Stone (Cintamani). Saint Jnaneshwar (1275-1296), wrote a commentary with 17 references to the Philosophers' Stone. The 7th century CE Hindu sage Thirumoolar, in his classic Tirumandhiram, explains humankind's path to immortality. In verse 2709 he declares that the very name of God, Shiva or the god Shambala, is an alchemical vehicle that turns the carbon-based human body into an immortal golden body.

The 16th CE century Swiss alchemist Paracelsus, who was believed to be the greatest alchemist of his time, wrote a 'how to' manual on the Philosophers' Stone entitled the *Archidoxa*. He believed in the existence of alkahest (a hypothetical universal solvent) which he thought was an undiscovered element that was the foundation of all of the other elements (earth, fire, water, air). Paracelsus believed that this element was, in fact, the Philosophers' Stone.

Swiss psychologist C.G. Jung's *The Secret of the Golden Flower* described Chinese alchemy as very similar to the alchemy of the West, especially as it dealt with the transformational symbolism of the human soul. He believed that the Taoists quest for immortality (the Golden Flower) was identical to the 'Philosopher's Stone,' which was the supreme objective of Western practitioners who wanted to understand the Great Art. Cher and I believe the Philosopher's Stone, like the 'Golden Flower' and Holy Grail legends, externalizes an interior power that we all have in common. We believe it's not something material at all. It's not a physical rock, gem, jewel, or gold nugget.

In my opinion, the Philosopher's Stone can transform human beings from mortal beings into immortal beings. Why? Because the Philosopher's Stone is the universal *Logoic Archetype* or life giving *Cosmic Logos* indivisiblized as us. We shall one day have highly alchemicalized spiritual bodies that are golden orbs of Pure Universal Consciousness. It'll mean purifying our physical bodies of their egocentric impurities and skin school attachments.

I believe the Philosopher's Stone is the *Cosmic Logos* aspect of the One Reality (Pure Universal Consciousness, God, etc.) within and as each of us, the *Cosmic Logos* expressing Itself as us, as you, as your children and grandchildren, as the person sitting beside you!

Planetary Consciousness

Planetary Consciousness recognizes that all of the stars, planets and galaxies in the Multiverse and the universes it spawns are living, breathing, conscious entities in their own right. This level of consciousness acknowledges that Gaia (planet Earth) and all of the celestial planets and systems throughout the universe are conscious and sentient beings which are composed of organisms that are all active cells with specific functions as parts of their particular bodies.

According to Gaia theorists, Gaia is a conscious being. For example, the eminent microbiologist Lyn Margulis, has shown how the vast rainforest, reefs, wetlands and even algae-ridden swamps of the Earth are actually the very organs of the body of Gaia; and the rivers are her arteries, and so on. There is also a constant exchange of energies occurring between our own bio-magnetic field and the geo-magnetic field of the Earth. It's this exchange of energies that links us to all other living things, and, indeed, to Gaia herself. This level of consciousness recognizes that we're actually 'organelles' of a single planetary cell in a living universe we call the 'Field.' Just as we are 'cells' of Gaia, she is a part of a solar system that's part of a galaxy which is part of a universe that is part of a Multiverse which is a cell within the *Field of Infinite Being.*

Polarity Paradox

People and organizations frequently have to choose between options that satisfy very different and often competing goals, sometimes mutually satisfying goals. This sets up what we refer to as a 'polarity paradox.' Ignoring a polarity paradox causes people and organizations to flip-flop between mutually desirable goals which widens the gap—that's the paradox.

Practicing the Presence

When you compromise your mental, physical, emotional, and spiritual health you dampen your ability to consciously become consciously one with the One. A dogmatic mindset, lack of physical exercise, anger, fear, unforgiveness, and religious myopia are all egocentric distractions that will keep you off center and out of balance. Practicing the Presence requires a distraction-free consciousness.

Applying the metaphysical knowledge and spiritual teachings that others have studied liberates them; applying the metaphysical knowledge and spiritual teachings that you have studied will liberate you.

What Brother Lawrence coined 'the Practice of the Presence' and Joel Goldsmith called 'Practicing the Presence' is what I call 'Actualizing the Presence' or 'Demonstrating the Presence' or 'Being the Presence out loud.'

Process Theology

According to Alfred North Whitehead, who developed the concept of Process Theology, it's an essential attribute of God (the *Cosmic Logos* attribute of the One Reality) to affect and be affected by temporal processes. This obviously is very much contrary to the forms of theism that hold what many people call God (the God meme) to be in all respects non-temporal (eternal), unchanging (immutable), and unaffected by the world (impassible). Process theology doesn't deny that God (the Universal Presence) is in some respects eternal (will never die), immutable (good all the time), and impassible (God's eternality is unaffected by actuality), but it contradicts fundamental religious views by insisting that God is in some respects temporal, mutable, and passible.

Proselytizing

The constant proselytizing of dogma is a indication of fear. The only argument with a proselytizer is a silent, but respectful retreat. The object of proselytizing isn't truth-sharing, but obnoxious and relentless persuasion.

Religious proselytizers are marathon athletes of the tongue who practice what I call tongue fu.

Prosperity

We must understand the spiritual dynamics behind manifesting something material from something immaterial. We must learn how to materialize what we want from the Field of Infinite Potential. What we want is here already—in potential—in the Field—waiting for us to call it forth by right of consciousness.

Lulls in prosperity are to be overcome, not for you to be overcome by their illusionary power.

There's no lid on what you can create. The secret is to know what you want. As you move forward on your own journey, and as you create your next chapter, take time to go into the Silence. Be still, and then determine what you want the future to look like for you!

Pure Universal Consciousness

Cher and I have a much different concept of God than what many people call God, because we don't believe in an anthropomorphic, white-bearded, white-robed God meme in the sky that micromanages everything down here in skin school. Our concept of God is more of an Energetic Presence which is the Ground of All Being and Nonbeing. I refer to It throughout this book as Pure Universal Consciousness, Infinite Isness, the One Reality, the Eternal Presence, the Field of Infinite Potential, the Source of All, etc. I am beginning to believe that the manifest and unmanifest realms (dimensions, fields, extensions) are gradations of Its dynamic super-energetic auras that are the effects of Its Indescribable and Unfathomable Essence.

ॐ ॐ ॐ

Quantum Chromodynamics

Quantum chromodynamics is the theory of a strong 'galactic glue,' quantum interactions (gravitational, electromagnetic, strong nuclear and weak nuclear) that describe the electrodynamics between quarks, antiquarks and gluons which make up hadrons such as protons, neutrons, pions and massless fermions. It turns out that asymptomatic quark-gluon plasma (quark soup) is one of the subatomic building blocks of matter that comes out of the 'Void.' I mention this theory because it speaks of the relationship between confinement and freedom, the magnetism of nonlocality, and no geography in Spirit. (See Apeiron reference.)

Quantum Exegesis

The 'Theory of Everything,' the Holy Grail of quantum physics, may always be just a 'TOE' wetting exercise in our attempt to understand the universe in which we live. I believe our quest to understand the 'nature of things—both quantum and cosmological—must be a combined scientifically empirical and spiritually revelatory path.

Quantum Intersection

As a spiritual being in a material universe you are a quantum intersection (composite) of an infinite number of interdimensional versions of yourself overlapping simultaneously in parallel universes, and perhaps even in parallel multiverses. That would suggest you are one of the multiplicity of interdimensional versions of 'you' that resides in a dimension 'out there.'

In order to maintain our transcendentalness we must nourish the part of us that wants to go its own way, that has a streak of rebelliousness at its core, a bit of outlawishness in its inner narrative. We must preserve the cantankerous part of us. It belongs to a larger transpersonal world than that is defined by our career goals, performance reviews, retirement accounts, or skin school experience.

Quantum Memory

The collective memory of all of the atomic and subatomic particles in the universe is called quantum memory. And that's important to know, because you are made up of quantum memory particularized as you.

Quantum Self

Your Quantum Self is your 'Karmic Akasha Database.' It's the composite of all of your past incarnations and/or reincarnations. (See a more detailed treatment of the Quantum Self in our book *More Straight Talk About Spiritual Stuff.*)

Question All Disconnects

Question all you have been taught at school, or church, or learned in books or workshops, and dismiss whatever diminishes your appreciation for your self-worth and innate *Higher Spiritual Nature.*

Quietism

I do not believe you'll achieve *Self-Realization* through quietism (omitting action). Your enlightenment will not be achieved through inactivity, idleness, or begging an anthropomorphic deity to do what it is your dharma to do. You free yourself by taking action, by cultivating a positive attitude in everything you do, by letting the divine powers act in you, through you and as you, which they unfailingly will do as soon as you remove the egocentric blinders that block their expression.

Qur'an

I thought I'd say a few words about the *Qur'an* through the eyes of a non-Muslim. The worldwide fear and distrust of our Muslim communities stems from the unconscionable actions and warped ideology of Muslim extremists who have abandoned their faith. The central teachings I believe that are contained in virtually every *surah* (chapter or section) and *ayah* (verse) of the *Qur'an* are: the *Qur'an* is a revelation from God, there is only one God who made heaven and earth, who is all-knowing and all powerful, merciful, loving, and has dominion over all things. Other recurring themes are that there will be a resurrection of souls; a final Judgment Day; those who live a life of kindness and compassion will receive rewards in the hereafter; and those who refuse to believe in the *Qur'an's* sacred scriptures will find nothing but torment in the fires of hell.

The orthodox Muslim view of the *Qur'an* as the Word of God, perfect and inimitable in message, language, style, and form, is strikingly similar to the fundamentalist Christian notion of the Bible's 'inerrancy.' If the *Cosmic Christ* is the Word of God made flesh, the *Qur'an* is the Word of God made text, and questioning its sanctity, accuracy or authority is considered an outright attack on Islam.

ॐ ॐ ॐ

Rage

Rage is the explosive agony of a highly emotional instant; but resentment can be the seething blunder of a lifetime. Like paint-soaked rags left in an attic too long, resentment that builds over time can suddenly burst into flammability when the right spark ignites it. It's better to extinguish the anger before you have to extinguish its volatility.

Rainbow

Mythologically speaking, the 'rainbow bridge,' or the 'shimmering path' as it's sometimes referenced, is seen as the celestial link between heaven and earth. The rainbow bridge was considered a pathway connecting humankind to the gods, and according to the Biblical account (which was most likely 'borrowed' from Babylonian mythology), the rainbow was God's promise to Noah never to flood the earth again.

However, in Babylonian mythology the Goddess Ishtar used her ethereal rainbow necklace to block God from receiving food offerings from humans, to punish God for sending the Great Flood to destroy her earthly children. In her book *The Woman's Encyclopedia of Myths and Secrets,* author, Barbara G. Walker, reports that the Biblical account mentioned above omits the Goddess altogether and conceals Ishtar's intervention on behalf of humankind.

In Norse mythology, Bifröst was the burning rainbow bridge between Midgard (the world) and Asgard (and the land of the gods). The Australian Aboriginal people believe the universe has two fundamental aspects – the physical world in which we live and an ethereal world called Dreamtime which underwrites the physical realm. In Aboriginal mythology, the Rainbow Serpent (one of the oldest life-giving motifs) is in the shape of the rainbow and bridges the physical and non-physical planes.

For some traditional native people including the Navajo and Hopi, the Sunbow (Whirling Rainbow) is believed to be a sign from the Great Spirit that marks the end of an era on Earth. This arc that resembles a rainbow around the Sun, reminds us to respect and live in harmony with all of the Creator's creations.

Now here's the science behind rainbows. Isaac Newton believed there were seven colors in the rainbow. Isaac Newton believed there were seven colors in the rainbow. Although, he admitted he could not distinguish well between colors, he confessed that because rainbows were special celestial phenomena they would have to have seven colors to correspond to the number of notes in a musical scale.

The human eye generally perceives six colors in the rainbow— red, orange, yellow, green, blue and violet. However, many people, including me, see indigo as a separate and legitimate color. In truth, there are many more 'rainbow colors' in the infrared and ultraviolet spectrums as well.

Rainbows are created by the diffused refraction of sunlight in water droplets. And the brilliant lit-up colors of the rainbow are created by the sun's photosphere. While each atom in the photosphere emits light at one quantum frequency, the doppler shifting of the light causes the lines to 'fuzz or blur' so that you see essentially a continuous spectrum of light. The strictly correct scientific answer for the number of colors that constitute a rainbow, would then be an infinite number of colors!

Rainbows are formed when water droplets in the atmosphere refract, or bend sunlight in just the right circumstances and at just the right angles. And you, as the awestruck observer, have to catch them at just the right angle to see them in their radiant rainbow glory.

Rainbows, scientists tell us, don't have a beginning or end because they are essentially circles in the sky. They only seem to connect with the ground because they extend below the horizon. And since you can't judge distance accurately from a distance, rainbows seem as if they touch the ground.

Here's another piece of scientific trivia. According to the National Center for Atmospheric Research, you must be positioned at exactly the right angle (42 degrees) relative to the sun's position to see rainbows. That fact also explains why all the rainbow chasing in the world won't get you to the 'pot of gold' at the end of a rainbow—or allow you to meet mythical leprechauns!

In fact, as far as scientists are concerned, no two people see the same rainbow—unless it's in a photo or in printed media. Why? Because the rainbow effect is entirely dependent on your own position and line of sight. That means that no matter how hard you try, you can never get close enough, theoretically, to see a rainbow's end—or beginning. (You notice I said theoretically)!

Although most people don't know it, a fainter secondary rainbow is often present outside the primary bow. Secondary rainbows are caused by a double reflection of sunlight inside each raindrop, and appear at an angle of 50–53°. And, if you've noticed, the colors of secondary rainbows are inverted relative to the primary bow. Neat huh!

The dark ribbon of unlit sky lying between the primary and secondary bows is called Alexander's band, named after Alexander of Aphrodisias who first described it. He was one of the most celebrated of the ancient Greek philosophers who wrote commentaries on—and bowed to—Aristotle's works.

Here's another interesting fact. The 50-53 degree angle of rainbows is also similar to the angle, or outer slope, of the Great Pyramid which is approximately 51.85 degrees.

Most of the ancient lure about rainbows sees them as a bridge or connecting link between heaven and earth, between gods and humankind. However, I have a different interpretation, a MetaSpiritual interpretation, because, as science has proven, rainbows float between heaven and earth— touching neither heaven nor earth! I believe they represent our spiritual unfoldment from the inside out and not a top down descension from on high—because rainbows don't come from 'up there.' They depend on our perspective 'down here.'

The rainbow is mentioned twice in the Bible: in the first book (Genesis 9:13-14), and in the last book (Revelation 4:3; 10:1). I've already mentioned the mythology surrounding the Genesis account. The Revelation account simply refers back to the Genesis story. MetaSpiritually, a rainbow represents our seven major etheralized spiritual power centers (chakras, the seven levels of consciousness, the 'many mansions' the *Cosmic Logos* as Jesus referred to) that must be quickened for us to achieve enlightenment.

The 'pot of gold' at the end of the rainbow motif isn't a material treasure. It represents our super-consciousness or Pure Universal Consciousness, the Philosopher's Stone (Alkimia), the Garden of Eden, and the Holy Grail.

Most of humankind has sought to find the 'pot of gold' at the end of the 'rainbow' in order to find health, wealth and happiness. In my opinion, the rainbow's real promise (*kundalini's* promise) and its treasure (enlightenment) will not be found in the atmospherics of material pursuits, but in the harmonics of our *Indwelling Cosmic Logos Consciousness.*

Reality

Humankind's concept of reality is built on the filters of the five physical senses. This sensory view of the world has always been inadequate and is, today, demonstrably invalid and even harmful when it is coupled with a sense-addicted consciousness.

Though quantum physics seems to deny the existence of a physical reality independent of its conscious observation, what if conscious observation creates everything—including ourselves—which would make our observations simply contextual and limited?

Reality is changeness and changlessness. One aspect of the One Reality is an empirical state of consciousness, the other is a nonempirical state of consciousness. One is a manifest state, the other an unmanifest state. One is atomic, the other subatomic. One visible, the other invisible. One is beinglessness, the other beingness.

Red Sea

You're probably familiar with the crossing of the Red Sea by the Israelites as they attempted to escape from Egypt. It's a story that has been glamorized by Hollywood on the big screen and one that's loosely based on a literal interpretation of scripture. I say loosely because the story of the Israelites flight is based on a mistranslation of the Hebrew word that means swamp, marsh or grass. The two words are *yam suph* which mean 'sedge, marsh grass, swamp or just plain grass' and not 'red.' *Yam* means water or sea. So, in the original Hebrew *yam suph* means reedy sea, sea of reeds or the reed sea.

Bible scholars who accept 'crossing the Red Sea' as an historical event have concocted many stories to justify how such a crossing could take place. Religious fundamentalists assert that their anthropomorphic God meme is all powerful and simply parted the Red Sea just like Charlton Heston did in the movie *The Ten Commandments.* Other scholars admit that the two Hebrew words describing the Red Sea in most Bible translations are mistranslations.

If the Israelites crossed the real geographical Red Sea they would have crossed at a narrow, low-lying, ankle deep salt water inlet located between Africa and the Arabian peninsula. This would make the Bible passage that says the Lord raised up an 'east wind' that pushed the shallow water off the bottom, so the Israelites could cross safely plausible. Unfortunately, the problem with that dubious scenario is there would have been three-to-six inches of mud for the Israelites to wade through. The probability of two million or more people with carts, flocks and herds crossing over this kind of swampy terrain in one night is highly unlikely. And, of course, it goes without saying that the Egyptian army's hot pursuit of the

Israelites would have come to an end when the wheels of their chariots bogged down and got stuck in the mud.

Some literalists assert that the Bible account notes that the water was like a 'wall' on both sides and that it 'covered' the Egyptians when they tried to cross. However, some scholars suggest that this passage is referring to the canyon area that is called the *Wadi Watir* which leads to the sea. The walls of the canyon (*wadi*) could have concealed their escape. Crossing the Red Sea at Nuweiba, as some scholars suggest, would have brought the depths of the Eilat Deep and the Aragonese Deep, each 3000 and 5000 feet deep respectively, into play. That's a lot of water to displace and nothing is mentioned of the flooding that would have occurred down stream when the sea 'walls' were put back together.

A few chariot wheels and wheels fixed to axels have been found on the sea floor at Nuweiba, as well as human and horse bones at the supposed crossing site. However, the few artifacts that have been recovered aren't enough to prove that thousands of Egyptian chariots and their military occupants met their fates when Moses stretched out his arm and commanded the waters to sweep over them.

I believe the Reed Sea (Red Sea) episode is an allegory of our continuing *Self-Realization* as we become more aware of our *True Divine Nature*. It's the story of our escaping from the bondage of a lower, more sense-soaked nature called our unenlightened ego.

'Crossing the Red Sea' requires leaving behind or transfusing a state of incarnated consciousness (egocentric consciousness). It means that since we have chosen another incarnate life, we have to 'wade through the sea of life' so we can 'land' on that 'farther shore' of a higher order of spiritual being. This symbolism is found universally in the wisdom (*vidya*) literature of the world's faith traditions. For example, Gilgamesh in the *Epic of Gilgamesh* has similarities to the Jonah story; and so does Jason and the Argonauts in Greek mythology; as does Oannes in Babylonian mythology; and Adapa in Mesopotamian lure, to name a few.

The 'sea' we all must cross without sinking too deeply in its waters is a 'sea' we must not get mired in or drowned in, because we are meant for the Promised Land (the Kingdom of God within us – our super-consciousness). In similar allegories, we are transported across a wide sea in a great fish's 'cabin' (remember the Jonah in the whale's belly story). Noah's ark floating above a sea of Flood waters is a similar analogy. MetaSpiritually, we are a great fish swimming about in the sea of physicality because we have chosen another human experience.

MetaSpiritually, the 'Red Sea' is our blood! On our journey toward *Self-Realization* we must leave our attachment to physical embodiment (which is composed of 'sea water'—our blood) behind and align ourselves fully with our Divine Nature, so we can free ourselves from the bondage of matter (the sea of material life). So far as we know we can 'leave our attachment to physical embodiment' in several ways: we can leave when we transition from our physical body through the conventional 'death experience,' and/or we can 'leave our attachment to physicality behind' while we are still embodied in a physical body that has become fully enlightened so we can materialize and dematerialize at will.

Essentially, we must transfuse our egocentric consciousness by transforming our blood (crossing over) into its true cosmic essence as the Vital Force that unites us with the Eternal Presence without incarnational attachments. Our temporal salineness (saltiness, human form) can be transformed into our eternal, highly alchemicalized spiritual essence (salt-free pure beingness, ethereal spiritual 'body') which shows that we have achieved full and complete *Self- Realization* with the One Reality. It means we can move in and out of material existence anytime we want to help the beings we find in that particular dimension achieve their *Self-Realization*.

Regeneration

Many varieties of insects land on larger creatures or objects in order to lick salty fluids off of them. Brave sweat bees land on the glistening arms, legs, faces and necks of people much larger than them to lap up salty sweat. Beautiful butterflies cluster like animated flower pedals around rims of bird baths in order to lap up salt residues. On our spiritual journey toward the farther reaches of the frontiers of consciousness we sip the nectar of the cosmos through our meditation and mystical experiences. It seems that living things share a taste for regenerative substances.

Reincarnation

Each reincarnation/incarnation can be a tithe to your enlightenment if you wake up during your skin school visit.

From a very young age I believed in reincarnation. My parents bought a new car every three years.

The reason repeated reincarnational experiences can be so detrimental to your soul growth is that you usually re-identify with the same or similar physicality of a previous skin school experience that imprints the old patterns and states of consciousness that caused you to reincarnate again in the first place. And as long as you keep on doing that you'll limit your spiritual growth. It takes considerable willpower to leave reincarnational experiences behind and choose not to repeat them. It's clear to me that reincarnational experiences are not a necessary condition for Self-Realization.

We're not in a state of exile for choosing reincarnational/ incarnational experiences. We never have been! We've simply limited our awareness sooo much that we can't see above our own Root chakra.

We have chosen the straightjacket of physicality over the wings of Spirit.

It you ask me, not that you have, but if you did, repeated reincarnations are just another way to procrastinate becoming enlightened.

Religion

My religion is Self-Realization (becoming consciously one with the One Reality through my Divine Nature). The closest I come to religion is being religiously spiritual. So, I consider my 'path' as MetaSpiritual. (See MetaSpirituality reference)

Religious worship of dogma is the funeral of giving scientific findings life after incontrovertible proof.

One of the drawbacks with mainstream religion is that it manages to coerce the spiritual instincts out of promising truth practitioners.

Mainstream religion is so pauperized by dogma and an exclusivity bias that any of its attempts at outreach show its calloused perspective. It has aimed too low. It continues to sell fear, guilt and shame as its "trinity of control" to bully believers into conformity, submission and mindless fiscal obedience.

Mainstream religion's fixation on dysfunctional dogma, mindless adherence to literal interpretations of scripture, and narcissistic pronouncements of doctrinal superiority continue to erode its relevance and intrinsic worth as a medium of enlightenment.

For many years I looked forward to looking back on the embedded theology of my youth and early adulthood. However, I'm thrilled to say that the MetaSpirituality I practice now doesn't have rearview mirrors. There's no need for them.

Most religious fundamentalists live on a carousel of dysfunction. Their fixation on the Bible's supposed inerrancy, an anthropomorphic goodie God meme in the sky, and women occupying subordinate roles has blinded the "faithful" into believing that the illusions they have spun are real and credible.

Frontal lobe deprivation keeps the 'faithful' in fear-based, guilt-ridden, dogmatized, limbic theology.

I feel about fundamental religious services the way I feel about diets. I don't participate in anything that starts with 'die.'

One of the problems Cher and I have with a one-channel religion (a religion based on the founder's teachings only) is its shortness of breadth.

Religious Exclusivity Bias

A religious exclusivity bias is characterized by believing a particular faith tradition is the only way to salvation. Unfortunately, religion's exclusivity bias derails it from its more spiritual and mystical roots, and thus, its enlightenment value. Until and unless it gets back on track, religion's exclusivity derailment will prevent it from reaching the station and status it could have.

Religious Fundamentalism

Religious fundamentalism is anti-Semitism dressed up as extremely corrosive Biblical literalism.

I'm not alone in my concern about the negative consequences of religious fundamentalism. Tenzin Gyatso, the 14th Dali Lama, reminds us, "(Religion) must be tempered by the insights and discoveries of science. If we ignore the discoveries of science, our practice is also impoverished, as this mindset can lead to (religious) fundamentalism." He's right, of course. Ignoring empirical evidence by remaining stuck in a dogmatic box is a recipe for 'spiritual cataracts' and a host of myopic, narrow-minded biases.

Religious Robotics

Mindless, brainwashed, automatized adherence to dogmatic religious principles that lead to habitual close-mindedness and lobotomized religious behavior is what I methodically refer to as religious robotics.

Rest

Read the following invitation and do what it says:

Close your eyes and listen for a moment. Sit motionless. Become aware of all the sounds around you. Keeping your eyes closed, gently press your palms over your ears. Sit motionless for several more minutes. Listen to the energy of your own body. Listen to the fascinating hum of yourself at rest. Listen to your saline oceanness!

Resurrection Consciousness

When you 'up your consciousness' the illusions and delusions of matter and the limitations of a finite human life experience become very evident. You realize that you are, and everything else is – one with the Infinite Presence (Pure Universal Consciousness, The Eternal Presence, the One Reality, etc.) many people call God. The 'stone of separation' has been rolled away as a result of your disciplined spiritual unfoldment. You have transcended the maya of separation. A resurrection consciousness means raising your base materialistic thoughts to their higher spiritual expressions; switching ego-driven ambitions to spirit-led aspirations; changing selfish motives to selfless service to others; and elevating your egocentric awareness to a *Cosmic Logos*-centric wholeness.

Reverence

Seek reverential moments everyday in spite of the fact that reverence is almost unheard of in a firecracker society where celebrity is measured in decibels and individual worth is determined by the size of one's stock market portfolio, amount of bling worn or kept locked up in a safe, the size of your house, the price of your car, the upper classness of your social network, and social status.

Rheostated Wisdom

There's amazing power in radiating wisdom (*vidya*). Your inner wisdom is like the rheostat on a dining room light. As you turn the rheostat clockwise, you're able to regulate the light – make it brighter. Turn it counter-clockwise and it dims. And even when you turn it all the way down, the potential for lighting the room is still there! When it comes to your innate wisdom you can also turn your 'rheostat' up or down. Your wisdom is there waiting to be used.

Right Thoughts

Right thoughts lead to right actions, so it's important to imprint those thoughts into your subconscious awareness, creating a muscle memory! That's why Cher and I recommend having a 'quiver' of strong, powerful affirmations at the ready, like muscle memory, when the temptation to give in to your human ego hits.

It's Not Rocket Science

The secret to mastering the art of living is not rocket science. It's aligning your waking consciousness with the *Extraordinary You* (your *Higher Spiritual Self*) before you do anything else, and you'll have the inner strength to do all you need to master the human experience. You'll be the beneficiary of: answers to financial concerns, career direction, inner peace, intuitive insights, the ability to challenge unquestioned answers, spectacular hunches, solutions to nagging family issues, phenomenal inspiration, deeper knowledge about truth principles, the ability to make wise decisions, and the strength to meet any skin school challenge.

It's not rocket science to realize there's something better than constantly worrying about the economy. It's not rocket science to realize there's something better than going through life with a debilitating habit or addiction. It's not rocket science to know that there's something better than being bored and burdened by meaningless routines. It's not rocket science to realize that there's more to life than debt; barely making ends meet; and the fear and doubt and disappointment which goes with a crazy economy. And it's certainly not rocket science to realize that there's more to you than meets the eye.

ॐ   ॐ   ॐ

Sabbath

Surrender to the sounds of silence. Take a portable sabbath. Turn the noise volume down of your day long enough to enjoy a few cubic feet of silence. Sequester yourself from the busyness and responsibilities of the day. Busyness isn't your jailer —your settling for the busyness is. Choose to be as busy as you want to be. Allow your inner peace and balance to shrink or expand in proportion to the quality of your choices. The more divinely focused your intentions and choices are the tighter your connection will be to the fantastic spiritual being you are.

Sacred Fire

The kundalini fire that lies as a coiled serpent at the base of the spine (Root Chakra) and rises through spiritual purity and self-mastery to the Crown Chakra, quickening the spiritual centers on the way, is called the sacred fire. It's characterized by its threefold flame nature: The sacred trinity of power, wisdom and love that's the manifestation of the sacred fire that takes up residency in the hearth center. (See our detailed MetaSpiritual treatment of the chakras in our book entitled *The Book of Revelation: New Metaphysical Version.*)

Sacred Places

The world offers us many famous spiritual spots: Jerusalem, Mecca, Delphi, Mount Arafat, the Black Hills, Lascaux, Bighorn Medicine Wheel, the Giant Serpent Mound, Stonehenge, Point Conception, Mount Sinai, the Ganges River, Machu Picchu, Niagara Falls, Victoria Falls, Mount Everest, Laurdes, Mount Olympus, the Great Pyramids, Mount Fuji, Mesa Verde, Canyon de Chelly, Ayers Rock, Enchanted Rock and Chaco Canyon, to name a few. We need to honor these holy places as symbols of our spiritual growth. We certainly need to keep them protected to remind us of their spiritual significance, yet we must see them connected with the rest of civilization and nature. They must remain integral with life's routines. Holy places are good reminders of our connectedness and oneness and contribute to our sense of heightened spiritual awareness, even a profound transcendentalness that envelops us when our five physical senses are involved. Our senses work better. We feel part of a larger and profound universal wholeness. It's important for you to know that holy places existed long before religions found them. How do I know? Because holy places are universal expressions of our collective divinity.

Look for the sacred in the ordinary; and when you find it you'll be on holy ground because your own oxygen footprint is holy ground. Each step you take is holy ground because you are an oxygen-based spiritual being.

Sacred Siddhi

Sacred *siddhi* means the perfection of all the physical senses and abilities that are inherent in the illumined soul. For example, perfection of sight means being able to literally see all the layers of the etheric fields and the subtler interdimensional realms of manifestation. Perfection of hearing means being able to telepathically tune into any level of sound, including the music of the spheres, and the other exquisite sounds intrinsic to creation at higher levels of vibration. The perfection of feeling means being able to feeeeel empathically the present, past or future physical and emotional states of others. The perfection of taste means being able to taste a substance without putting anything in your mouth. The perfection of touching means being able to touch objects and perceive information about the article and its owner. The *siddhic* journey starts with disciplined mindfulness to perfect in-the-moment living.

Sacred Spiritual Language

A sacred spiritual language that doesn't have religious connotations, anthropomorphic undercurrents, denominational biases, or patriarchal overtones is evolving because people all over the world are seeing themselves as more spiritual than religious. And that's wonderful, because when our consciousness elevates to a higher spiritual octave, there needs to be a language that complements that growth.

It appears we can learn something from humpback whales when it comes to languaging our experience. T. Lehmann and other researchers have found that humpback whales alter their songs every year between breeding seasons. One year all humpback whales sing the same song and the next year they sing a different one—and the changes aren't random. The songs are modified during the breeding season as their oceanic experiences change. Both whales and us humans, then, are constantly changing their communication system to accommodate the changes in their environments and life experiences. As a matter of fact whales and we humans are the only two species that are believed to change their language—although dolphins and some species of birds are now thought to modify their language too.

Saintly Joviality

Feel your way around your somberness, seriousness, and formality long enough to allow humor to soften your rough edges. Your rigidness can become a subconscious straightjacket that protects the raw edges of your insecurities from being exposed. Unfortunately, this impenetrable veneer steals the joy, glee, and merriment out of your life unless you get serious about softening your seriousness.

Satan

The religious belief that there is an evil personage called satan, also referred to as the prince of darkness, that rivals an anthropomorphic God meme in the sky for our souls, is an absurdity that has been perpetuated for far too long. It has evolved out of an abject denial of our innate divinity and our collective refusal to take responsibility for severing the spiritual ties that reveal our true origin as human expressions of the Eternal Presence (Pure Universal Consciousness) in physical form. So, in order to conceal our true nature humankind has created a convenient scapegoat to blame for its chronic indiscretions.

Schlepped Self-Care

Schlepped Self-care means taking better care of our automobiles, stock portfolios, fishing rods, plasma TV's, iPads and iPhones, and bling than we take care of ourselves, and especially our *SuperSelf*™. It means neglecting the vocabulary of our body, mind, and soul while expecting to gain balance and peace of mind. It means failing to consciously and consistently align our human self (egoic soul, jiva soul, *dak dzin*) with our *SuperSelf*™ (*Divine Self, Authentic Spiritual Self, Logos Nature, Higher Spiritual Self*).

Scripture

In any written scripture, regardless of the faith tradition, the white space ahead, behind and between the letters represents the truth of the Eternal Presence (Pure Universal Consciousness). The letters and words simply represent one interpretation (approximation, collapsed wave, particle, limitation) of the expansive and limitless 'white field' of possibility (the Eternal Presence).

Secret Chamber of the Heart Center

The secret chamber of your heart center is a spiritual chamber behind the heart center (Heart Chakra) surrounded by cosmic light and protection. It's the connecting point of the Silver Cord of crystal light that emanates from your 'I Am Nature' to sustain the beating of your physical heart and the life in your body. It brings life, purpose, cosmic integration and stability to your earthly body. It's the place that connects you with your timeless and indestructible Divine Essence.

Selfhood

As you experience each dimension of being on your way to Selfhood, you must not allow your rootedness in each dimension to trump your *Self-Realization*.

Self-Worth

We sell our divine inheritance for a mess of pottage when we settle for 'worship' instead of 'worthship.' (See Worthship reference.)

Sentient Consciousness

According to a host of scientists from a variety of disciplines, all species—from bees, earthworms, octopuses, ravens, and crows to magpies, parrots, tuna, mice, whales, dogs, cats and monkeys—are capable of sophisticated, learned, non-stereotyped behaviors that are associated with sentient consciousness. Their constitutive proteins, genes, synapses, cells and neural circuits are as sophisticated and as specialized as human biosystems. Consequently, the weight of evidence indicates that we humans are not unique in possessing the innate neurology that generates consciousness.

Non-human animals have the neuroanatomical, neurochemical, and neurophysiological basics of conscious states along with the capacity to exhibit intentional behaviors—even seemingly spiritual behaviors. This level of Pure Universal Beingness expressing Itself as Sentient Consciousness is a mosaic of sentience and intellect, and seems to be conscious of its collective connection with Gaia, we humans—and do doubt with the cosmos itself!

Sermon on the Mount

The Sermon on the Mount probably never happened. It was probably a remastered update of two Hebrew Testament writings to sell Yeshua (Jesus) as the New Testament arbiter of the new world order. It was most likely patterned after the eight 'blessed' stanzas in Psalm 119 and an elaboration of the 10 Commandments of Moses (which may have themselves been based in part, on the Egyptian *Papyrus of Ani* and the *Code of Hammurabi* that were written three centuries earlier).

Serpent's Lie

The serpent's lie is a misnomer fabricated to support an original sin theology. The serpentine energy is our Inner Wisdom (*vidya*) telling us that the Real Spiritual Us (our Divine Nature) does not die. What does die, when we become fully illumined, is our divinity-denying egocentric nature that we have allowed to block our enlightenment. However, the 'serpent' does 'lie'—it lies curled at the base of our Root Chakra, waiting for us to awaken our kundalini energies for their trip up our spinal column to the Crown Chakra which precipitates our full enlightenment.

Second Coming

The 'second coming' I'm referring to is this: Most New Thought people who realize they are spiritual beings having a human experience fail to tap into their higher spiritual, rare psychic, highly intuitive and supernatural powers, because they never venture far enough on their 'first wind' to enjoy the incredible aliveness and energy of their 'second wind.'

When we are born into a human experience for the first time, that's the 'First Coming' of our Higher Spiritual Nature into physical form in that particular incarnation as us. When we realize we are the Cosmic Logos expressing Itself as us in that particular incarnation, we experience a 'Second Coming.' During our repeated reincarnations and incarnations we will experience many 'comings into the realization that we are the Eternal Presence expressing Itself through the *Cosmic Logos* as us' during our soul journey toward our own *Self-Realization*.

Secular City

Your egocentric consciousness, with its materialistic bent and self-aggrandizing nature, is the 'secular city' you have built in consciousness to foster the illusion of separation from your I Am Nature (*Higher Spiritual Self*) while you're matriculating through your skin school experience.

Self-Awareness

According to the research, there's no neuro-receptor that distinguishes any gradation of the color of gray or grayness. That being said, there's no gray area when it comes to our real relationship with the One Presence (Pure Universal Consciousness) expressing Itself in human form as us. You either have that awareness or you don't.

As far as we know there are at least 100 billion neurons that make up our neural real estate. I'm going to ask you to hold on for a moment because neuroscience guesstimates are changing as fast as our materialistic interests. When you place 302 neurons in a petri dish and interconnect them, they become a nervous system that can keep the worm *Caenorhabditis* elegans alive—sensing the invertebrate's surroundings, making decisions and issuing commands to the worm's body. Interconnect 100 billion neurons— with 100 trillion connections—and you have yourself a human brain, capable of much, much more. This number matches the various guesstimates of the number of stars in our galaxy. In one calculation, the Milky Way has a mass of about 100 billion solar masses. So, it makes sense from that standpoint to translate that to 100 billion stars. Theoretically, this accounts for the stars that would be bigger or smaller than our Sun (which is deemed to be an average-sized star), and averages them out. Other mass estimates bring the number of stars from 400 billion to over a trillion. Isn't this galactic and molecular mirroring awesome! What a universe 'out there' (I'm pointing to the stars in the night sky) and 'in here' (I'm pointing to my head).

There's a spiritual connection involved in doing what we love and in loving what we do. That connection is a contrast between our human self and our *SuperSelf*™ (*Higher Spiritual Self*). It's written in the language of love and its terms are only contingent on our willingness to "follow our bliss." So, I'm going to ask you: What brings you joy? What do you love to do? What are you doing about it? The more you examine these questions, the more you'll realize whether you are living on purpose or mindlessly wandering.

Self-Disclosure

I'm very much a fan of *Self-disclosure* (admitting that you are the Eternal Presence as the *Cosmic Logos* expressing Itself in human form as you). Sooooo, Self-disclose! Affirm your divine origins! Celebrate your innate divinity.

Self-Improvement

Cringe-worthy slips are thoughts, choices and actions you have initiated that are totally uncharacteristic of you. They're probably missteps you haven't shared with anyone else because you feel embarrassed to have had them. They include blasphemous statements, expletives, and obscenities that belittle your divine connection; selfish choices that tarnish your image of yourself; and foolish actions that stain your truth walk. Hopefully they're simple slip-ups and can be corrected with conscientiousness, a little tact, and a lot of soul searching. Recognize them for what they are and clear your consciousness by creating powerful denial statements (denying their power over you), along with their accompanying affirmations, to cleanse cringe-worthy slips from your thoughts, feelings and behaviors.

Self-Mastery

You must remember that your living in this flesh and blood curriculum called skin school doesn't have to be at the mercy of matter. You'll achieve self-mastery when you achieve *Self-Mastery.*

Self-Realization

Self Realization is obligatory, and will continue to be obligatory in whatever dimension we find ourselves. Our *Self-Realization* comes from knowing our *Higher Spiritual Self*—not 'no-ing' our *Higher Spiritual Self* —so that we know we are the Great I Am (Eternal Presence, the One Reality, the Infinite Isness, the Arche, Pure Universal Consciousness, etc.) expressing Itself in human form as us.

Senzar

Senzar is a mythical language or 'mystery speech' of initiated adepts all over the world. It's purported to be a very ancient mystery language from Atlantis, and the etymologically predates Sanskrit. I believe there may have been such a language, but it was lost when Atlantis was lost.

Separation Anxiety

We experience separation anxiety every time we reincarnate, each time we have an error thought or make a poor word choice, every time we choose a material thought over a spiritual intention, each time our materialistic actions belie our spiritual and ethical values. The emotional disconnect we feel in each of these experiences retails the separation anxiety that surfaces, because we are out of alignment (oneing) with our *True Spiritual Nature* which is divine.

The Sevenfold Vow

The Sevenfold Vow, from a MetaSpiritual perspective, is the strong inner prompting to open each of the seven major chakras in order to traverse the Sacred Path (the energetic journey up our spinal cord). (See Sacred Path reference in *More Straight Talk About Spiritual Stuff* book.)

Shaktipat

Shaktipat or *Śaktipāta* is Sanskrit for 'psychic energy to transmit' and refers to the channeling of spiritual energy from one person to another. *Shaktipat* can be transmitted with a sacred word, mantra, short affirmation—or by a look, thought or physical touch focused on the recipient's Third Eye. *Shaktipat* can also be transmitted face-to-face or at a distance, through an object such as a flower or fruit or even by phone, text or letter. It's a form of ceremonial energy transference and remote healing. It's similar to the esoteric 'overshadowing' which is a voluntary cooperative process in which the charisma of a Master Teacher's consciousness influences the physical, emotional and mental states of a disciple.

Shambhallah

According to Tibetan Buddhist, Hindu, Chinese, and Theosophical esoteric traditions, *Shambhallah* is a mythical ethereal kingdom that hovers just above the earth. Its teachings and healing practices are eons older than any of our organized religions.

Its inhabitants are ascended spiritual masters whose purpose is to help heal humanity and to lead us to high levels of spirituality, enlightenment, oneness and loving kindness.

However, Cher and I believe that *Shambhallah* symbolizes humankind's collective super-consciousness which its highest state of consciousness in human form. It 'hovers' over 'earth' (our ordinary state of consciousness) which is generally ruled by our unenlightened ego. In addition to the seven major chakras and forty-two minor chakras that are attached psychically to our body, Eastern mystical traditions tell us that there are other chakras outside our body. For example, one of those energy centers (chakras) is a transpersonal chakra called the Soul Star Chakra. The Soul Star Chakra is believed to be located approximately six inches above the Crown Chakra at the top of our head. It's white and gold in color. Called the 'seat of the soul' it's the psychic bridge between our soul and the soul of the universe.

Once all seven of our major chakras are awakened the Soul Star Chakra connects those energies with the cosmos, allowing our alchemicalized body to travel inter-dimensionally. Another one of those external energy centers is called the Earth Star Chakra, also called the Super Root Chakra, is believed to be located approximately 12-18 inches below the bottoms of our feet and connected psychically to the soles of our feet. It's usually brown or dark brown in color and connects us with the magnetic core of the Earth. (See *Life-Changing Spiritual Practices, Vol. 5* on our website: The CenterForSpiritualAwakening.com)

Side-Piercing Spear Wound Archetype

The Side-Piercing Spear, also known as the Spear of Destiny, and the Lance of Longinus, is the name given to the spear that pierced the side of the Cosmic Logos (referred to as the Christ in Biblical literature) as Yeshua (Jesus) as he hung on the cross, according to the *Gospel of John*. You may be curious about other 'spear-piercings in the side of world savior' myths and their possible connections to the Christian Christ myth. I'll start with the Christ myth as recorded in the New Testament.

Three of the four gospels (Matthew, Mark and Luke) neglect to mention a Roman centurion using a spear to pierce Jesus' side, which resulted in water and blood pouring out. Why did they omit this important incident? Interestingly, the 'spear piercing the side of Jesus' incident seems to have been added for the specific purpose of identifying Yeshua (Jesus) as the Jewish savior. It's clear that in some of the ancient cultures in the era of and before the Roman Empire, there were sacrificial saviors who were portrayed as having been 'wounded in their side.'

For example, the Scandinavian gods Odin and Marsyas of Mindanao were said to have been hung on a tree and stabbed with a spear just as Jesus was said to have been crucified and pierced by Longinus' spear. Vishnu and Krishna (who was supposedly pinned to a tree by arrows), were both thought to have been crucified saviors stabbed in the side. Google their stories.

In the ancient Norse text the *Havamal*, one of the Norse *eddas* (a collection of Old Norse poems on Norse legends) contains a poem called the *Runatal* (stanza 138), which quotes Odin as saying:

"I know that I hung, on a windy tree, for all of nine nights, wounded with a spear, and given to Óðinn, myself to myself, on that tree, which no man knows from what roots it runs."

What's even more interesting is that, Odin's beloved son, Balder, is pierced with a spear of mistletoe. Balder dies like Jesus did in the New Testament story, and like Jesus in Revelation, Balder will be reborn or resurrected in the time of the *Ragnarok* or the Norse 'apocalypse' to destroy evil once and for all. (Looks like an archetypical story, doesn't it!). Moreover, as Jesus is seen as the 'Light of the World, so Balder is the 'god of light.' So, like Jesus, Balder is the savior of the world who brings peace. And, similar to Jesus who had 12 apostles, Balder is depicted as having 12 knights as protectors.

The Christ motif is universal. Christ, means 'the anointed one' and is a term applied to Attis, Adonis, Tammuz, Osiris, and many other pre-Christian gods. Even the name 'Christ' is a variation on KRST (Horus, the Anointed One) and Krishna (Christna or Christos in Bengali) thousands of years before the Christ as Jesus walked the Earth.

In his book *The Bible Fraud*, author Tony Bushby reminds us:

*The word Kristo and its derivations, Krst, Krist, Kristo,
Khyst, and Krishna, all appeared in every ancient religious
system. The original Kristo concept was believed to be the
personal and invisible mediator and guide between God and
everything spiritual in man. The Krist concept has been an
ancient religious tradition continually suppressed by the
Catholic church through the centuries.*

Here's some interesting facts that would describe a spear
piercing someone's side whether that person was the Cosmic Christ
as Jesus or any other of the world saviors who suffered the same
fate. I'll use the Jesus event as the archetypical example of the
universal metaphysical meaning of having one's side pierced with
a spear or lance. I believe you'll find this information interesting
indeed:

Two aspects of Jesus' death are sources of great controversy,
even to this day. They are the nature of the wound in his side and
the cause of his death after only several hours on the cross. Some
scholars attribute the flow of water to be ascites (the accumulation
of fluid in the peritoneal cavity) or urine, from an abdominal
midline perforation of the bladder. However, the Greek word *plvra*,
(or pleura) used in John's Gospel clearly implies the rib area being
involved. It seems probable to me, given that scenario, that the
wound was in the rib cavity behind the breastbone and adjacent to
the thoracic vertebra, which would place the wound well away
from the abdominal midline. That's just simple human anatomy.

Although the side of the body in which Jesus was reported as
suffering the wound was not specified by John, it traditionally has
been depicted as occurring on the right side. That makes sense,
because a large flow of blood would be more likely with a
perforation of the distended and thin-walled right atrium than the
thick-walled and contracted left ventricle. Although the location of
the wound will most likely never be known with certainty, the right
side seems more probable than the left for the reasons I outlined
above. It's a matter of biology.

In all due respect, some of the skepticism in accepting John's
account stems from the difficulty in explaining, with medical

accuracy, the flow of both blood and water. Part of this difficulty is based on the assumption that blood appeared first, and then the water. However, in the ancient Greek texts, it seems likely that the writer of John's Gospel was emphasizing the prominence of blood and not its appearance preceding the water.

If you'll allow me a few more 'side ways' comments. J Physiologically speaking, the water probably was serous pleural effusion (the fluid-filled space that surrounds the lungs) and amber-colored pericardial fluid. That means it would have preceded the flow of blood and would have been smaller in volume than the blood. What's more, because of Jesus' impending heart failure, pleural and pericardial effusions may have developed and would have added to the volume of the apparent loss of water. Also, the blood, could have come from the right atrium, the right ventricle, or even from the hemoperieardium (blood in the pericardial sac of the heart).

Many Biblically oriented physiologists believe that Jesus died of cardiac rupture. Clearly, the weight of historical and medical conjecture indicates that Jesus was probably dead before the wound to his side was inflicted. And that seems to support the traditional view that the spear, thrust between his right ribs, probably perforated not only the right lung, but also the pericardium and heart, which would have ensured his death.

My conclusion is that 'side-wounding and spear-piercing' stories are universal archetypes. They point to something fundamental in the human condition! The spear piercing may even point to humankind's dynamic divinity represented by the mythical 'first couple'—Adam and Eve! I'll explain later with a rather 'piercing' statement.

I'd like to cover one more point before I conclude this spear-piercing snapshot. From a purely pragmatic and mechanical standpoint the centurion used his spear to pierce the side of the itinerate preacher to make sure Jesus would die sooner. However, from a deeply spiritually and allegorical perspective I'm going to elaborate on the promise I mentioned earlier about the mythical 'first couple' which I believe ties the spear-piercing myth to the Adam and Eve myth.

According to Jewish tradition, Eve was produced from Adam's rib. However, MetaSpiritually speaking, I believe it means that all creation occurs when the Cosmic Life Force (Spirit's vertical dimension) morphs into matter (the horizontal dimension) and forms a right angle at the point where the two vibrations meet.

The result of this cosmic penetration is symbolized by the human skeleton which features the spinal column and the ribs that are at right angles at their junctures. (By the way, when you stand straight with your legs together and your arms extended shoulder level high, your body is in the shape of a cross. I'm just saying). Eve, representing universal feminine energy, is formed (set free) when the horizontal arm (rib) of the allegorical human cross meets the descending (materializing) energy of the One Reality as It morphs into physicality.

I can extend this allegory by suggesting that the mythical spear represents a second horizontal influence which is the product of a self-aggrandizing ego that wants to ensure its temporal rulership. It wants to make sure that not only our spiritual dimension dies, but the dynamic dimension of the eternal feminine energies will be prevented from being released as they were at the 'birth' of Eve.

Since we spiritual beings morphed into human form and arrived on the planet, our extremely paranoid egocentric nature has sought to silence both our divine impulses and our highly intuitive Eve qualities which epitomize the heart-centered awareness that symbolizes the highly nurturing, wisdom-centered, keenly subjective, unconditional love-oriented, right-brained, social and emotive nature of our make-up.

Our unenlightened ego, which is the product of our morphing into matter (the empirical realm), wants to repress our Divine Nature and keep our heart energies subordinate to our intellect. The spear (the piercing nature of our self-aggrandizement) in our side (the heart of our human personality) is the recalcitrant ego's weapon of choice to ensure its dominance over our human personality. However, the same mythical couple story surfaces in almost every faith tradition—the transforming power of our Heart Center as it resuscitates our Heady Nature and the resurrecting power of our Divine Nature which guides us toward our eventual *Self-Realization*!

Silver Cord

The silver cord, also known as the *sutratma* (life thread) of the *antahkarana* (the connnectivity between your waking mind and your super-consciousness) is the life-giving Pure Universal Consciousness linkage from your ethereal body to your physical body. If the silver cord is severed, your consciousness can no longer be 'stepped down' to your physical body. Esoteric and mystical traditions describe the silver cord as a sort of umbilical cord, ethereal leash, or a long elastic cable made of light or energy.

There are many interpretations of what the silver cord is, how it functions, and what it looks like. For example, some believe the silver cord refers simply to our spinal marrow. Others describe the cord as a wispy, etheric-looking filament about one inch in diameter which is silvery-grayish in color. Most see it as having infinite elasticity, stretching as far as the Vital Body (the alchemicalized Etheric Body that is the spiritual body we use during and between incarnations) can travel. Yet other teachings hold that although the cord not only serves as a link between the two bodies, it also limits the Vital Body from wandering too far.

The Ecclesiastes account (12: 6-7) references the cord which is loosed; and the bowl, pitcher, and wheel which are broken. These four items seem to be associated with our graduation (transition) from skin school—according to the mainstream religious perspective which believes in death. MetaSpiritually, the loosened cord refers to the severed silver cord; the golden bowl reference represents the broken connection with our super-consciousness (*Self Consciousness*); the broken pitcher is our physical body which has been disconnected from the silver cord; and the broken wheel symbolizes the end of our current incarnational experience.

Single-Pointedness

Single-Pointedness or nowness (hereness), is sometimes referred to as the fourth moment or Samadhi. It is a state of non-ego. The Tibetan term for this is *lhakthong dagme tokpe sherap*, which means 'the knowledge of egoless insight through penetrative awareness.' It's the well-disciplined spiritual practice of holding your attention (focus) without being distracted. It is a tranquil abiding and emphasizes a sort of 'mental fushion' where focusing on a specific object (thought, concept) is the goal. The 'objects' I generally concentrate on are 'impermanence, limitlessness, oneness and nonlocality.' I must tell you that disciplined practice is the key. The amount of time you choose to engage in one single-pointed sitting is up to you. However, it should be enough time for you to become proficient in single-pointedness without undue distractions. You'll find that this experience gives you a seamless openness unconfined by space or time so that you not only feel your connectedness with your Higher Spiritual Nature, which is your ethereal dimension, but you experience yourself as a extension of the Pure Universal Consciousness, which is known by many names.

Sins of the Fathers

In Exodus 20:5 the often repeated genealogical threat that the "sins of the fathers shall be visited upon the children unto the third and fourth generation," if interpreted literally and referring to actual human fathers and children, has unfortunately been used to condemn generations of innocent children and families with the stain of guilt and shame caused by their 'fathers.' MetaSpiritually interpreted, this verse refers to the karmic effects of a succession of reincarnations of a particular person (man or woman) whose previous incarnation's thoughts and actions (fathers) follow him or her in subsequent embodiments (children) and carry karmic baggage that cause illnesses in those later incarnations (generations).

This interpretation helps clarify the issues surrounding a newborn infant or adult later in life who suffers an unfortunate and 'unfair' illness which begs the question: "What did he or she do to deserve this awful illness?" The current soul most likely didn't do anything to 'deserve' the illness. However, his or her thoughts and actions (fathers) in a previous incarnation caused him or her to be the 'beneficiary' of the current unexplained malady. The important teaching is that we must expiate as much negative karma as we can in each lifetime to reduce and even eliminate the karmic baggage carried from one lifetime to another.

Slaughter of the Innocents

The slaughter of innocent children reported in the *Gospel of Matthew* was probably borrowed from Jeremiah 31:15 when the children in the Northern Kingdom were killed by the Assyrians. The New Testament story of the killing of the innocents was written in (added) to promote how close the New Testament messiah had come to annihilation as an infant just like the children in Jeremiah's time had been close to death. It also sounds very much like the Old Testament story of how close the infant Moses had come to being killed, but was rescued by Pharaoh's daughter. (Exodus 1:15, 16). In both cases, MetaSpiritually speaking, the infant Moses and Jesus accounts represent our being able to rise above the negativity and limitations of our human experiences (Moses, drawn up from the riverbank; Jesus, protected by his parents who fled from Herod) by affirming—and then seeing—the opportunities present when we 'up our consciousness' to a higher spiritual octave.

Sleep Your Way Into Enlightenment

The cosmic dimensions of sleep lead to your ultimate awakening and illumination because sleeptime slows your outer physical senses down enough to allow you to connect with the inner you, your True Spiritual Nature. The 'cellular you' and the 'ethereal you' have the opportunity to connect, unimpeded by the externally-oriented ego.

See sleep as a powerful mind, body and soul spiritual practice that connects you with the Field of Infinite Potential.

In addition to meeting your physiological, mental and emotional needs, sleep also contributes synergistically to your spiritual needs. For example, you can enter a dream state and receive guidance from the dream world and then 're-set' your conscious awareness to accommodate the goodness of the dream content. You can also use the content of both the hypnagogic (your state of consciousness during the onset of sleep) and the hypnopompic (your state of conscious during the onset of wakefulness) insperiences (all internal states of consciousness) as catalysts for your continuing soul unfoldment.

So, in addition to reducing overhead and lamp lighting, I invite you to consider turning off your TV, iPads, Kindles and Nooks, smartphones and computers 45 minutes to an hour before bedtime. Reduce the amount of room lighting, poorly circulating indoor air, late night processed foods, and highly dramatic late night TV shows and movies. Make sleep a priority. Cool the room temperature to 66 to 68 degrees Fahrenheit. I'm not kidding! Overconsumption of light and overconsumption of information fill your body with immense amounts of energetic clutter to process. When you add the cumulative effects of the day's events into your cluttered electronic environment, your 'insomnia quotient' skyrockets.

I wish I could say that all it takes is a good mattress, the right pillow and a glass of wine to get a good night's sleep. But just like there's no short cut to enlightenment, there's no quick fix to get the sleep you need. Lifestyle changes are a must to reap the rewards of a deep, spiritually synergistic sleep.

Be aware that thoughtful, synergistic sleep turns the heuristics of external experiences into growing-edge insperiences that are transformational and soul deepening.

The cosmic dimensions of sleep will lead to your ultimate awakening and illumination, because sleeptime slows your outer physical senses down enough to allow you to connect with the inner you, your True Nature. The 'cellular you' and the 'ethereal you' have the opportunity to connect, unimpeded by the externally-oriented, materialistic ego.

Son-day

Many churches are accustomed to the term 'Sunday' which references both the day of the week and the day set aside for worship services. Sun or Sol represents the solar deity and for Christians is considered a pagan perspective. So, perhaps the day set aside for Christian worship services should be called Son-day for the Son of God and not Sunday for sun god Sol—I'm just saying.

Soul/Oversoul

The Quantum Self (the composite of all of your past reincarnational selves and concurrent parallel universe selves) which underwrites each of your physical states of being, is your Oversoul (the sum total of your previous selves and your current human personality). (See Quantum Self reference and the other Quantum Self references throughout this book.)

Soul Intoxication

Soul (the human personality) intoxication means becoming inebriated (thoroughly engrossed) in the whirlpool (sense pleasures) of matter.

Soullessness

Anyone who professes concern about the welfare of others but remains unconcerned about the poverty that damns them, the social inequalities that bury them, the economic conditions that strangle them, the built-in dangers they face, and the prejudices that disenfranchise them is speaking from a value-corrupted position. Forgive me if that sounds a bit harsh, but you no doubt know, or have heard of, soulless people like that.

Soul Retrieval

Soul retrieval is the process of reclaiming some forgotten part of ourselves that fragmented and separated from our Vital Body (Ethereal Double) as a result of a serious past life trauma. Retrieval takes place when a lost fragment or aspect of our soul is remembered and becomes an epiphany in our current skin school experience. A profoundly moving experience in most instances, soul retrieval brings us into wholeness once again. In a very real sense, the lost fragments are the orphans that we have created by mistrusting, rejecting, condemning, judging, cursing, neglecting, or even suppressing an experience that results in a separation from ourselves (psychic tear). The root cause of soul fragmentation is denying—not facing—the truth about ourselves. It can take many incarnations to achieve soul retrieval or only our current incarnation if we have the courage to face a difficulty or serious life challenge head-on.

Soul Spelunking

Soul Spelunking means having an interest in the dynamics and exploration of your various levels of consciousness (your subconscious, waking conscious, super-conscious, altered states of consciousness, dream states, past lives, multidimensional states of being, etc.). The exploration focuses on your small 's' self stuff (your *Quantum Self* incarnational material) in order to understand who and what you really are. (See *Quantum Self* references.)

Soul Worth

Religious fundamentalism preaches pusillanimity (faint-heartedness, mousiness, timidity) when it comes to exploring esoteric and metaphysical truths. However, one of the chief tenets of our MetaSpiritual perspective is *magna animasness* (daring, confidence, great courage, fearlessness, gallantry). Pusillanimity sells fear, shame, conformity and original sin. MetaSpirituality invites oneness with your Divine Nature, your limitless human worth, your worthship and eternal goodness. (See Worthship references.)

Spanda

According to the Spanda Foundation, "*Spanda* is the original, primordial subtle vibration that arises from the dynamic interplay of the passive and the creative polarizations of the Absolute, and that by unfolding Itself into the energetic process of differentiation brings forth the whole of creation. It's the creative pulse of the universe as it manifests into the dynamism of living forms … On the transcendental plane, *Spanda* is the pulsating radiance flashing forth of the Absolute consciousness who appears as the universal source and essential form of the Absolute's own energetic self-expression." (See ^{The}Word reference.)

"*Spanda* is the pulsation of the ecstasy of the divine consciousness" (*Abinahavagupta*, 950-1016 CE, Kashmirian mystic and philosopher).

Spanda is the Cosmic Logos expressing Itself in physicality as both sentient and insentient beings, worlds, universes, multiverses, and megaverses.

Speed of Light

According to the International Astronomical Union the presumed speed of light in a vacuum is 299,792,458 meters per second. That means it takes sunlight about 8 minutes 17 seconds to travel the average distance between the Sun and the Earth. MetaSpiritually speaking, light is only the amperage of our awareness of who we are and our relationship to the universe and our *Cosmic Logos Essence*. Our super-consciousness is a gazillion times faster than the speed of light. It only takes us a nano-second to realize we are 'here' (I'm referring to Earth) and the Sun is 'there.'

Spider Silk Surgery and Spirituality

Spider silk is very elastic (it can even be used for violin strings). It conducts heat as well as metals and, by weight, is tougher than silkworm silk and steel. *Spidroin* is the main structural protein in spider silk. One gram of the protein produces about 5.6 miles of artificial silk—enough to make hundreds of silk screws that can be used for bone fractures. Isn't that incredible! The threads make good stitching material because of their very high tear resistance, tensile strength, and particularly smooth surface.

Researchers are looking into more applications of how the fiber in spider webs can be used to help connect new nerve fibers and veins in us humans. The spider fiber could change how surgeons treat wounds. The higher consciousness message is that we must see the medicinal value and symbiotic nature of the interconnectedness we have with all living things as one of our primary quantum fields of study. This kind of relationship with living organisms and biosystems is part of the spirituality of wholeness and oneness that unites us in consciousness with the universe. (See Dogs Smell Cancer and Diabetes.)

Spiritual Anthropology

A person's spiritual growth evolves over time. It's filled with what I call 'artifacts of awakening.' For example, our journey is initially characterized with basic socio-cultural behaviors like feeling part of an 'in group,' fixation on the literal interpretation of scripture, and adopting dogmatic religion as the 'narrow path.' This pre-enlightened path is covered with chards of intolerance and disrespect for other faith traditions, doctrinal and ceremonial exclusivity, the strongly established denominational bond of 'born again' kinship, fossilized adherence to the inerrancy of Biblical scripture, and the remains of an anthropomorphic God meme that has long been shown to be the adornment of preliterate religious groups. (If I had more space I'd tell you how I really feel about the fundamentalist religious perspective). However, I'll say this, once we get away from the superficial 'digs' of pediatric religious studies, our excavations into our evolving spiritual consciousness become more mature and expansive, propelling us toward a new era of spiritual, not religious, growth.

Spiritual Being

When you call yourself a Christian, or a Catholic, or a Buddhist, or a Hindu, or a Jew, or a Muslim, or a Baha'i, or American, or European, or Asian, or by any other religious or regional affiliation, you're contributing to the excesses, prejudices, parochial world views, and addictions associated with those labels. Can you see that? You are 'guilty by association,' as the saying goes. Why? Because you're separating yourself from the rest of humankind. The thing is, when you separate yourself by nationality, religious preference, belief system, socio-political persuasion, and cultural tradition, you are, in a very real sense, perpetuating the excesses and prejudices identified with that label, either consciously or unconsciously. Suppose you referred to yourself simply as a 'spiritual being who, like others, is having a human experience' when you meet people. Just think what you could do with that introduction to ameliorate the ills of the world!

Spiritual Cemetery

A consciousness composed of repressed (unexpressed, discarded, neglected, silenced) spiritual thoughts, insights, principles, and inclinations is a spiritual cemetery. You can identify it by the political, nationalistic, cultural and regional tombstones that mark the burial sites of its prejudiced viewpoints which have buried any hope of oneness, unity and collective welfare.

Spiritual Discipline

Discipline your 'self' (your egocentric human self) so that it aligns with your '*Self*' (your *Divine Nature*, your *Higher Spiritual Self*). Devote (subordinate, apprentice, calibrate) your 'self' to your '*Self*' as your primary spiritual practice.

The more consistent the deviation, the more acceptable it becomes. So, stop dissing your True Spiritual Nature and cultivate a disciplined spiritual practice.

Continue to be disciplined in your MetaSpiritual studies. When someone ridicules you with their obnoxious 'ha-ha's,' stay focused on your 'aha's' of Self-discovery.

Spiritual Growth

You can't measure spiritual growth with a material yardstick. Many of the Buddhist teachings are simply Buddha-ful!

What distinguishes spiritual people with high levels of personal mastery is they have cultivated a higher level of rapport between their human self and their Higher Spiritual Self.

Your human self is just in apprenticeship to your Higher Spiritual Self.

You'll never grow in your spirituality if you try to move left and right, and backwards and forward at the same time.

A *forelsket reaction* is the euphoria we feel when we first come across a compelling spiritual truth and see its implications for transforming our lives. Forelsket is a Norwegian term that refers to the euphoria we experience when we first fall in love. It prompts you to remain a student of awe and wonder. It pulls you toward newness, uniqueness and novelty. It tempts you toward freshness and surprise. It's the elation, exhilaration, glee, and bliss you feel toward high-falutin' MetaSpiritual principles and teachings that'll keep you interested—and deepened—as a truth seeker and practitioner.

Here's a thought: Nothing is interesting, especially if you're interested in nothing.

I never let seminary, ministers' conferences, New Thought workshops or church services interfere with my enlightenment.

There are still plenty of spiritual, metaphysical, religious and scientific interpretations to be made as we increase our collective awareness of who and what we really are—and our relationship to one another and to the universe which we have made our home away from Home. And when you come across fanatically asserted dogmatic biases of any kind, I hope you'll realize how nonsensical it is to rigidly defend those dogmatic restraints by rolling over backwards with hoots and howls of good-natured laughter. I make that a practice, by acknowledging it to myself or having a good belly laugh, because we're all trying to make sense out of the universe and discover our place in it—AND everyone, including me, has a right to their BS (belief system)!

> *Make your spiritual growth not just a passing moment,*
> *but composed of permanent now moments*
> *of lifetime devotion.*

No one should swallow whole the spiritual perspectives of another without giving thought to what is shared. We must allow the sharing of spiritual and religious perspectives to clear a path and open a dialogue that leads to mutual growth, transformation and expansion.

Make the most of your spiritual growth and the least of your material whims.

Seeds sown from our higher consciousness and nourished through study, meditation, prayer, service to others, and a regular spiritual practice can bring us a bumper crop of mind-boggling awarenesses!

Spiritual Highways

The *Bible, Torah* and *Talmud, Qur'an, Bhagavad Gita, Tripitakas, Rigveda* and other *Vedas, Upanishads, Kitáb-i-Aqdas, Kojiki, The Agamas, The Book of Rites,* and *Guru Granth Sahib* to name a few, are great highways of religious guidance. Their combined exoteric, esoteric and metaphysical teachings can constitute great religious and spiritual highways of spiritual enlightenment.

Spiritual Impoverishment

Deeper parts of us, that come from the depths of our soul, rebel against the sterility and superficiality of scriptural literalism, the notion of scriptural inerrancy, and age old patriarchal heresy that has led to the majority of humankind's spiritual impoverishment.

^Your^ **Spiritual IP Address**

Your spiritual IP address is the amazing *Cosmic Logos Presence* (your *Higher Spiritual Self*) expressing Itself as you in human form. It is the Eternal Presence, the One Reality actualized as your *Higher Spiritual Self*. You are a continuation of this Universal Presence as a physical being. You can imagine anything you want, be anything you want, have anything you want, go anywhere you want, see anything you want, hear anything you want, taste anything you want, smell anything you want, think anything you want, feel anything you want, intuit anything you want, create anything you want, do anything you want, travel anywhere you want in any dimension of being you want, and manifest anything you want by right of your *Higher Spiritual Consciousness.*

Just so I'm clear, your human ego is not your Spiritual IP Address! Your egocentric nature is finding it difficult to get back Home. When you subordinate your unenlightened ego to your Divine Nature through a variety of spiritual practices, especially the insperience called meditation, you'll find the 'Interstellar Voice' that will lead you Home again.

Part of the problem with our worldly ego is that it suffers from what I call 'separation anxiety.' You experience separation anxiety every time you reincarnate, each time you have an error thought or make a poor word choice, every time you choose a material thought over a spiritual intention, each time your materialistic actions belie your spiritual values. The emotional disconnect you feel in each of these experiences retails the separation anxiety that surfaces, because you are out of alignment (phase, calibration) with your True Nature which is divine.

Without an awareness of your True Divine Nature much of your time is spent keeping chaos at bay, protecting your life and property, staving off financial disaster, climbing longer and longer corporate ladders, and managing the conflicts and disappointments that invariably find you. Emotional avalanches and mud slides crash against you. You turn molehills into mountains, and create avalanches of fear and doubt that bury you. You mistake assumptions as facts and half-truths as gospel. No wonder you get confused. And once you're confused by molehills, you usually run into mountains of doubt and valleys of discontentment.

Your egocentric consciousness, with its materialistic bent and self-aggrandizing nature, is the 'secular city' you've built in consciousness to foster your illusion of separation from your I Am Nature while you're matriculating through your skin school experience.

I call the 'secular city's' antics schlepped Self-care. Schlepped Self-care means taking better care of your automobiles, stock portfolios, fishing rods, plasma TV's, iPads and iPhones, and bling than you take care of yourself, and especially your *SuperSelf*™. It means neglecting the vocabulary of your body, mind, and soul while expecting to gain balance and peace of mind. It means failing to consciously and consistently align your human self (egoic soul, jiva soul) with your *SuperSelf*™ (*Divine Self, Authentic Self, Logos Self, Higher Spiritual Self*).

Actually, you can 'be' Home anytime and anywhere you want, because your Spiritual Home's IP Address is a nonlocal state of Higher Super-Consciousness (nonlocality doesn't have a zip code).

It has been called by many names: Heaven, the Kingdom of God, Paradise, the Philosopher's Stone, the Promised Land, Arcadia, Nirvana, Shangri-la, Elysium, Utopia, Cosmic Consciousness, Pure Consciousness, the Field of Infinite Potential, the Garden of Eden, the Sacred City, Universal Realm, Realm of the Absolute, etc.

Spiritual Narcolepsy

Most people are sleepwalking their way through skin school totally unaware of their Divine Nature—that they are the human expressions of the Pure Universal Consciousness expressing Itself in quantum form as them.

Spiritual Practice

Because MetaSpirituality is a way of life, it invites you to use a multiplicity of religious practices and turn them into spiritual practices, so you turn outer-focused religious practices into inner-focused spiritual ones.

Choose spiritual practices that work for you. Mindlessly adopting a practice someone else recommends isn't nearly as important as how you feeeel while you're engaged in it. Be willing to "try out" a number of practices. Look for a good fit between the practice and you. When you commit to a practice see it as one of the ways to express your spiritual unfoldment. Make it high on your lifestyle priority list. See it as concrete evidence of walking your talk.

How many people live on the spiritual principles they say they have? You can't build a spiritual practice on what you intend to practice. Disciplined spiritual practice will remove the doubts and fears and worries that theology can't solve.

Too much theology and too little practice is trying to eat the menu instead of the meal.

Spiritual education, affirmative prayer, meditation (and other insperiences), healing, developing our youth, a consciousness of giving, using affirmations and denials, kindness, compassion, unconditional love, forgiveness, practicing the Noble Eightfold Path, practicing the Hindu paths to *Self-Realization* (the path of liberation, the path of devotion, and the path of knowledge and philosophy), practicing the Jewish paths of (*tshuvah* – repentance, *tzedaka* – charity - and *gemilut hasadim* – kindness, etc.), studying Baha'i scripture, *salat* (an Islamic prayer ritual), Unity's Twelve Powers, integrating meaningful spiritual perspectives from other faith traditions, visualization, metaphysical interpretation of scripture, MetaSpiritual teachings, conscientious study and application of scientific findings which complement growing-edge spiritual perspectives, and loving service to others are just a few spiritual practices you may want to consider on your higher consciousness journey. (See the ten volumes of spiritual practices on our website: TheGlobalCenterForSpiritualAwakening.com)

One of our chief spiritual practices is honoring the MetaSpiritual principles we teach no matter what skin school experiences we face.

Your spiritual practice will shrink or expand in direct proportion to your devotion and commitment.

Your spiritual practice is the accumulation of the in-the-moment decisions you make to honor your divine genealogy.

Spiritual Principles

Spiritual principles can never be weathervanes, spinning first this way and then that way, with the shifting winds of doubt, fear, materialistic whims or expediency. Spiritual principles are compasses. They point toward your *Higher Spiritual Self.*

Here's a minister's take on Spiritual Principles and church leadership: There's no surer way to be disliked by a church board than to honor the Truth principles you teach when board members forget the Truth principles they've learned.

Sharing Truth principles is both opium and utopia for me.

Hesitation and procrastination are forms of doubt holding on longer in order to delay applying spiritual principles.

In my opinion, inconsistently practicing the spiritual principles you know is a misdemeanor. Neglecting to practice them at all is a felony.

Stereogramming

Have you ever seen a 3-D stereogram picture? It's a picture hidden within another picture that just looks like a design—but when you stare at it for a while, a new image forms. It's truly amazing! I believe this is a perfect example to illustrate how, with a little effort, we can see more clearly. We get so confused by the trivia and trivialness of the world of appearance, when the Truth is there all the time, just waiting for us to SEE MORE CLEARLY!

So, how do we see things from an enlightened perspective? Here's a simple technique: Play the Hidden Picture Game With Life. Whenever you find yourself in a difficult situation, when things appear to be falling apart, or just going totally haywire, STOP. Go into the Silence and affirm that what you are experiencing is just INFORMATION. It's simply the confused rhetoric and cluttered hyperbole of the world of outer appearances. Within this seemingly cluttered picture there is peace; there is joy; there is good; there are answers. Affirm: I SEE through the eyes of an enlightened spiritual perspective!

"Straight Is the Gate and Narrow Is the Way"

MetaSpiritually, this scripture in Matthew's Gospel (7:14) refers to the narrow 72 centimeter trip of your kundalini energy (the Holy Spirit) up your spinal column. The mileposts along the way are your seven major chakras. (See the Ark of the Covenant reference in this book and the 72 Centimeter Path and the Sacred Path references in our *More Straight Talk About Spiritual Stuff* book.)

Straight Talk

If you want to know the the truth, my unplugged 'straight talk' book is just another way of my keeping a diary.

Subconsciousness Sense

Think of your subconscious mind as the storage room (dark data warehouse) of everything that is currently not in your conscious mind. Your subconsciousness (dark data wearhouse) stores all of your previous life experiences, your cognitions, your beliefs and memories, all of the images you've ever seen, every thought and emotion you've ever had, all of your inclinations and intentions, and so on. It's the repository of your dreams, and, in Cher's and my opinion, it includes the 'multi-generational dark data' of your previous lives and reincarnational experiences in a timeless part of you we call your Quantum Self. (See the *Quantum Self* references throughout this book.)

I'm inviting you to become more subconscious conscious because, psychologists tell us that your subconscious doesn't know the difference between fiction and what's real. It takes things literally! The subconscious mind doesn't perceive the dualistic reality we experience with our five senses. As far as psychologists know, our subconscious doesn't know the difference between good and bad, big and small, up and down, the smell of chocolate and chocolate itself. And this is one of the things that makes it an immensely powerful state of consciousness, subconsciously speaking, of course.

Sukkotic Courage

This *sukkotic* courage idea was inspired by the Sukkot festival which is the Jewish harvest celebration. Sukkot are hut-like structures that the Israelites lived in during their 40 years of travel through the wilderness after they drastically downsized the Egyptian labor force. By analogy, as temporary dwellings, the sukkot could very well represent the belief that even though all existence is fragile, we can persevere and turn trials into triumphs. They could also represent our physical embodiments during our incarnational and reincarnational experiences.

Suicide Wraps

In the rodeo industry, a suicide wrap is a particular rope wrap bull riders use when wrapping the bull rope around their hand. The wrap allows the cowboy enough leverage and staying power to remain aboard a bucking horse or steer. However, it's very difficult to get out of a suicide wrap if the cowboy falls off the animal. That, of course, causes a serious problem for the rider who becomes vulnerable to the hooves and horns of a bull with a bad attitude. From a higher consciousness perspective, suicide wraps mean wrapping yourself around false teachings, false assumptions, and false beliefs that can delay and/or 'kill' your chances of achieving enlightenment. For example, any religious tradition that builds fear into its teachings, adheres to fossilized dogma, champions an anthropomorphic God meme in the sky that punishes some and rewards others, discriminates against people who are different, and retails a cataclysmic end to the world is selling suicide wraps. Unfortunately, suicide wraps are not being barred from mainstream religious teachings, thus making more pre-enlightened thinkers vulnerable to the hooves and horns of religious fundamentalists who want to marginalize any teachings that are more spiritual than religious.

Being jerked around by any false teaching that refuses to allow you the freedom, respect and dignity you deserve to gain higher spiritual understanding and transcendental awareness is higher thought suicide wrapped in ecclesiastical clothing.

Super-Abled

Cher and I consider those who value, study and apply universal metaphysical truths in order to live a prayer-conditioned, higher thought-enhanced, and spiritually centered life as Super-abled – and those who devalue and even reject metaphysical and esoteric thought as dis-abled when it comes to actualizing their True Divine Potential.

Super-Consciousness

Allow your super-consciousness (the loclized the Kingdom of Heaven, Infinite Field of Potential, Pure Universal Consciousness) to shed light on your waking consciousness (your egocentric consciousness). When you do this, you'll experience a super consciousness lift!

Symbelic Toasts

Symbelic toasts are of Germanic Neopagan origin and are ceremonial toasts to the gods, heroes and ancestors of their religion with an alcoholic beverage. The primary elements of *symbelic* toasts are drinking ale or mead from a drinking horn, making speeches (which often include formulaic boasting and oaths), and gift giving. Any oaths made are considered sacrosanct and become part of the destiny of the oath giver. I use this *symbelic* toast idea as a metaphor for what I call 'Hidden Manna Toasts' and toast the hidden manna I receive with affirmations of appreciation for having connected with my *Higher Spiritual Self.* The drinks I use are non-alcoholic: water, unsweetened peach and mixed berry tea, citrus juices, etc. (See the Hidden Manna reference.)

Synthetic Happiness

When we accept something we get, even when it's not what we initially wanted, we usually still feel satisfied and content with the choice. Synthetic happiness can be as enduring as "natural happiness" that occurs when we get what we wanted in the first place. I often think about the impact of synthetic happiness when I consider our choice as spiritual beings to experience another human incarnation.

Although we want to experience what the oneness and transcendence feels like in our relationship with the One Universal Presence as 'incarnation-free' beings, we still choose the duality and illusions that are associated with our incarnation into skin school, and evidently feel satisfied with the synthetic happiness that comes with it. I can say that with a clear conscience, because I'm here again—in skin school!

Syzygic Sabbaticals

Syzygic sabbaticals mean divinely ordering the alignment of your mind, body, and soul with your *Higher Spiritual Self* so you can eliminate the following influences from your life: absurdity, aggrandizement, agitation, alcoholism, anger, bitterness, blind ambition, callousness, corruption, cruelty, demeaning comments, drug addiction, envy, excessive excess, excuses, fear, filth, gluttony, greed, hatred, harshness, hostility, hurtfulness, hypocrisy, idiocy, immorality, incompetence, indecency, insincerity, jealousy, laziness, litigation, littering, maliciousness, manipulation, materialism, narcissism, negativism, neglect, nit-picking, over-indulgence, paranoia, passivity, pessimism, prejudice, profanity, quarrelsomeness, resentment, redundancy, repugnancy, rhetoric, rudeness, scuzziness, self-centeredness, self-doubt, shortsightedness, snobbishness, substance abuse, thoughtlessness, tokenism, toxic behavior, underhandedness, unfounded suspicions, unsportsmanlike conduct, unnecessary pain, violence, wastefulness, wolfishness, workaholism, and spiteful yakkity-yak.

Syzygy is a term used by psychologist Carl Jung which means synergistic alignment. The implication is to align your human self with your *Divine Self* by eliminating error tendencies and behaviors. As you can see from the list of error tendencies above, this 'sabbatical' practice is a daily practice. It demands constancy of purpose and awareness to become the best spiritual being you can be.

ॐ ॐ ॐ

Thanksliving

Thanksliving places you above the ups and downs of everyday living. It's a life in which you are not held captive by outer appearances. It's a life of perpetual gratitude. A life of being grateful for what you have. A life of great fullness.

Thanksliving means you are the curator of your own soul when you elevate your thinking to a higher spiritual octave. It means allowing your inner priesthood to guarantee safe passage through the crucible of your skin school experience—no matter what happens to you down here. Your thoughts, intentions, beliefs, cells and molecules are monks, nuns and priests. Your body is your monastery and your consciousness is your cathedral.

Be *'thanks full.'* It turns a meal into communion, an ordinary moment into an extraordinary moment, a house into a home, a stranger into a friend. Being thankful turns unemployment into redirection and the unknown into an adventure. It turns disappointments into acceptance and confusion into clarity. It turns hard times into the best of times, a handshake into a hug, a smile into laughter, being scared into sacred beingness, anger into forgiveness, unhappy employment into ecstatic other employment, relocation into opportunity, illness into illumination.

The 'TH' Factor

The 'TH' Factor is putting 'there … here.' It's turning 'worship' into 'worthship.' It's turning religious exclusivity and separation from the Eternal Presence into spiritual inclusivity and oneness with the One Reality. It's taking a 'heeling' position behind an anthropomorphic god perspective and transforming it into a 'healing' Universal Consciousness perspective which assures you that you are the One Reality expressing Itself through Its *Cosmic Logos Nature* in human form as you.

What I'm describing is a profound cosmic interconnectedness (entanglement, unanimity, indivisibility) which underwrites both your true finite and infinite natures. You don't have to worship anything, especially an anthropomorphic God meme in the sky! All you have to do is understand, accept and honor your innate worthiness as a spiritual being having a human experience. (See Worthship reference.)

Theophysical Treks

Theophysics is a merger between theology and physics. It's a branch of religious theology with the aim of proving the existence of a higher Universal Reality (the Eternal Presence, God, the All, the Infinite Isness, etc.) using quantum physics arguments.

The Third Eye

The Third Eye (Inner Eye, All Seeing Eye, Seat of the Soul, the Eye of Dangma, the Eye of Siva) is a mystical and vestigial organ that is essentially the invisible pineal eye that gives us perception beyond ordinary sight. It's an inner sight that we all possess! In certain dharmic spiritual traditions such as Hinduism and Taoism and in MetaSpiritual teachings, the Third Eye is expressed as the Brow Chakra. The Greek word *Enoichion* literally means 'the eye of the seer' or 'third eye.' So, you can see, the 'third eye' mythology has been around a long time.

The Third Eye is the etheric gate that leads to inner realms of higher consciousness. In MetaSpirituality, the Third Eye symbolizes a high state of enlightenment in which the mental images that are expressed have deeply personal, psychological and spiritual significance. The Third Eye is associated with mystical visions, clairvoyance, chakra and auric sensitivity, precognition, astral travel, and out-of-body experiences.

The Christian Bible itself alludes to pinecones and the pineal gland in several accounts, sometimes quite specifically. For example, in Genesis 32:30-31, Jacob wrestles all night with an angel, and is commanded to change his name to Israel. The passage then reports the following: "And Jacob called the name of the place Peniel: 'For I have seen God face to face, and my life is preserved.' And as he passed over Peniel the sun rose upon him." (The Hebrew translation of the word 'Peniel' means 'face of God, vision of God, recognition of God, and understanding of God).

The biological center of the Third Eye is the pinecone-shaped pineal gland which is located in the geometric center of our brain and attached to the Third Ventricle. It lies between the two hemispheres, tucked in a groove where the two rounded thalamic bodies join. When it's opened, its etheric energies extend to the middle of our foreheads, slightly above the junction of the eyebrows. It's believed that we had, in far ancient times, an actual Third Eye in the back of the head with physical and psychic functions. Over time, as we evolved, this eye atrophied and sunk into what today is known as the pineal gland, its neural embodiment.

It's been called the 'seat of the soul,' 'the 'mind's eye,' 'the 'gateway to non-dualistic thinking,' the 'inner highway to clairvoyance,' the 'avenue to wisdom,' and the 'thoroughfare to higher consciousness.' In Plato's Republic, it's described this way: "... in (all of us) there is an Eye of the soul which … is far more precious than ten thousand bodily eyes, for by it alone is truth seen … The Eye of the soul … is alone naturally adapted to be resuscitated and excited."

In the kundalini yoga tradition, it's believed we can awaken the Third Eye by activating all seven of our major chakras. The kundalini energy must be summoned to the forehead, where it expands and then awakens the Third Eye. The energy travels along the *ida* (left channel) and *pingala* (right channel), up the central pole or *sushumna*. This is the process esoterically depicted by the caduceus symbol of two antithetical snakes spiraling up a central staff. (See Chakraology reference.)

Tilling the Soil

Gardening, landscaping, the tilling of the soil are the earthy extensions of our mental gardening, creative hemispheric landscaping, and the tilling of the soil of our consciousness. Planting flowers, scrubs and trees mirrors the planting of spiritual teachings and principles in our conscious awareness. Both are natural processes. Both need tending, nurturing and growth. Both are disciplines of faith. The make-up and constitution of earthy soil and the cosmic dimensions of your consciousness are both dynamic receptacles to produce a Garden of Eden-like potentiality. MetaSpiritually, the Garden of Eden is your super-consciousness (*Self-Realized Consciousness*). It's the realm of 'divine soil' within you that spawns divine insights and ideas. It's a limitless realm of possibility and expansiveness. All you have to do is grow it by keeping an open mind, move beyond dogmatic perspectives, and feeeeeel your oneness with your innate divinity.

Time Warp

The gravity of our descent (morphing, metamorphosizing, remodeling, shape-shifting) into matter has not only caused us to live in a time warp, but a consciousness warp. The pull of sensory experience has kept us bound to this incarnational experience and increased the 'wait time' for our enlightenment.

Tochis Path

Tochis is a Yiddish word that means 'rear-end, posterior or butt.' Postponing your spiritual growth means sitting lethargically on your posterior instead of methodically and enthusiastically applying the truth principles you know.

Torah

The *Torah* is the law of God revealed to Moses covering Genesis, Exodus, Leviticus, Numbers and Deuteronomy (Pentateuch) and the other nineteen books of the *Tanakh* (the Christian Old Testament). The scriptures that are used in Jewish services are written on parchment scrolls. They're always hand-written, in attractive Hebrew calligraphy with 'crowns' (crows-foot-like marks coming up from the upper points) on many of the letters. This style of writing is known as STA'M (an abbreviation for '*Sifrei Torah, Tefillin* and *Mezuzot*).

Torch of Truth

A particular design of the 'torch of truth' is associated with the Dominican Order. The torch is often shown being carried in the mouth of a little black and white dog. It's believed to have originated in a dream St. Dominic's mother had when she was pregnant with her son who was later to become a saint. She dreamed of her child as a little black and white dog which illuminated the world by carrying a torch in his mouth. There seems to have been no gray area in her belief about her son.

Trauma Triage

Construing the silver lining in trauma is trauma triage! Psychologists tell us that people who move through the stages of trauma—from languishing to survival to recovery to thriving—believe their lives have improved because of their positive response to tragedy: they seem to find guilt-free solace; renewed appreciation of the preciousness of life; and perceive that they can and will be stronger for responding courageously in the aftermath. By analogy, in each of our skin school appearances, we have a built-in 'silver lining.' It's called our *Logos Nature (Higher Spiritual Self)*. And It's connected to us by the mystical Silver Cord.

Tree of Life

The allegorical Tree of Life is the eternal, fohated, Pure Universal Consciousness which underwrites all beingness and non-beingness. Its 'roots' are said to be firmly placed in the firmament of the Eternal Isness and Its 'canopy' extending into the realm of physicality. *Fohat* is a Tibetan term for the energetic or motion aspect of Pure Universal Consciousness. It is *Spanda*, the connecting link between Spirit and matter that causes manifestation. In the Secret Doctrine it's referred to as the 'principle of perfectibility.' *Fohat*, like *Spanda*, translates (transforms, morphs) archetypical ideas and cosmic forces into material form.

The 'trunk' of the Tree of Life, MetaSpiritually speaking, materializes as our spinal column and spinal cord. The treelike canopy of 'spreading branches' manifests as our central and peripheral nervous systems; and the 'flowers' are actualized as the spiritual energy centers called chakras. The 'fruits' of the nervous system are the various nerves like the optic nerve, retina, cranial nerves, olfactory nerves, etc. (See our *Spiritually Speaking Glossary* for a detailed treatment of both the Tree of Life and the Tree of the Knowledge of Good and Evil)

Trinity

The trinities I've adopted for my spiritual growth are: the *Arche, Spanda* and *Apeiron*—metaphysics, science and philosophy (the three features of MetaSpirituality)—Pure Universal Consciousness, *Cosmic Logos* and Holy Spirit—meditation, forgiveness and loving kindness—challenging all unquestioned answers, open-mindedness and esoteric teachings. (See the references to the *Arche, Apeiron,* and *Spanda* in this book and the *Arche, Apeiron,* and *Spanda* references in our *More Straight Talk* book)

Trust

When you have absolute trust, no explanation is needed. When you don't have trust, no explanation is good enough.

Trumpet Symbology

The 'voice' (sound) of the trumpet, according to ancient metaphysicians, when fully emitted, focused and directed is a powerful cosmogenic force (primordial creative energy). Empedocles, a respected pre-Socratic philosopher, originated the cosmogenic theory of the dynamic interaction of the four universal elements: fire, air, water and earth. The result of the concentrated breath (Cosmic Word) and contained expiration, the entire trumpet vibrates and emits a note (sound) that is symbolic of intense creative energy that can cause the growth or collapse of manifested elements that contain the four universal elements. The power of the expiration creates a 'singularity of sound' that allegorically represents the power of the 'Word' to call into expression Spirit's effect on matter. This concept is similar to the 'spanda' concept in Kashmir Salvism's conscious energy philosophy pertaining to the 'creative pulse of a newly-formed universe. (See the *Spanda* references in this book and the detailed *Spanda* reference in our *More Straight Talk* book.)

Truthology

Cher and I believe that those who choose not to search for truth—whether it be historical, political, spiritual, quantum, neuroscientific, or biological truths—will remain at the margins of conscious awareness. Because they have not given much thought to it, they'll more than likely find it difficult to distinguish truth from fiction and appearance from reality.

I've found that the Truth will always
call your bluff!

Cher and I decided long ago that we must teach MetaSpiritual truths at all times—and if necessary, use words.

Truth Principles

When you get to it, I would like you to read the last statement in this paragraph aloud. Before you do, though, raise your right hand. Now place your right palm over your right ear. The reason I have you do this is because what you are about to read is so important for your health, wealth, and happiness that I don't want these words going in one ear and out the other! Are you ready? I'm going to trust that you've honored my instructions and placed your palm over your ear: Your spiritual growth and human happiness are not so much limited by unanswered questions as they are unquestioned answers!

You will not fully understand deeper truths from a neck-up-only perspective.

Truth Practitioners

All truth practitioners, whether their journey to higher consciousness takes them through Mecca, Jerusalem, Allahabad, Amristar, CERN, Fermilab, the Himalayas, the Space Station Mir (while it was orbiting), NEEMO (NASA's underwater laboratory called Aquarius) are in good company as they take advantage of manmade structures in their search for the One Reality which is the Ground of All Being and Non-being. Fortunately, the most seasoned – and enlightened – seekers of Self Realization are not bound exclusively by the sacred texts of their upbringing: the *Bible* for Christians; the *Torah* for Jews; the *Qur'an* for Muslims; the *Guru Granth Sahib* for Sikhs; the *Vedas, Upanishads*, and *Epics* for Hindus. The monumentally fortuitous thing about courageous truth practitioners—the thing they have in common—is their election to expand their thinking past the literal interpretations of their respective faith traditions and soar into the esoterical and metaphysical "cloud of knowing" that will someday revolutionize human thought and raise our collective human consciousness *(anima mundi)* to its highest spiritual octave.

Speaking the truth is not the same thing as bringing the truth 'up there' down here and sharing it with those who either seek it or need to know it, even if it's an inconvenient truth. People hearing the truth must 'up their consciousness' to be willing to understand the truth. Otherwise, the higher thought frequencies will be misaligned and all that will be heard will be good-intentioned philosophical noise.

Truth Triptych

Aligning (entraining, calibrating) ourselves with our *Higher Spiritual Self* through visualization, meditation, affirmative prayer, positive affirmations, metaphysical study, a consciousness of giving, unconditional love, kindness and compassion, and eternal optimism are all important connecting flights on our Truth Triptych to *Self-Realization.*

Tube of Light

The tube of light houses the white light that descends from the heart of the I Am Presence in answer to our earthly sojourn. Reported to be about nine feet in diameter, it's a cylinder that emanates from the I AM Presence and materializes just above our head as the Soul Star Chakra and extends three feet below our feet as the Earth Star Chakra. The tube of light is believed to shield us from negative energies and is sustained twenty-four hours a day as long as harmony is maintained in our thoughts, feelings, words and actions. (See the Earth Star and Soul Star Chakras spiritual practices in Vol. 5 of our *Life Changing Spiritual Practices* book.)

Twin Pillars

Two pillar symbolism can be found in the esoteric traditions of many religions and esoteric orders and was not exclusive with the Hebrews. The pillars usually appear at either side of the entrance to initiation chambers and temples. Since the dawn of civilization, the entrances to sacred and mysterious places have been 'guarded' by two pillars.

In the traditional Biblical account when the Israelites fled Egypt, their God took the form of both fire and a cloud: "And the Lord went before them by day in a pillar of cloud, to lead them the way; and by night in a pillar of fire, to give them light; to go by day and night. He took not away the pillar of the cloud by day, nor the pillar of fire by night, from before the people" (Exodus 13:21-22).

The manifestation of the deity in Hebrew history as a pillar of clouds and a pillar of fire points to the earlier origin of the two pillars in Vedic conceptions of the divine presence. Thus, the Hebrew symbol of a pillar of cloud by day and of fire by night refers to the same natural objects – clouds and fire – that were symbols of the presence of the deity according to ancient Vedic traditions.

Hiram, the architect sent by King Hiram of Tyre to build Solomon's Temple, cast a pair of hollow bronze pillars that stood on the outer portico of the temple. One was finished in silver and the other in gold and studded with emeralds. Standing in the north, the pillar of silver represented the 'Pillar of Smoke' and was called Boaz, which signifies strength. Standing in the south, the pillar of gold and emeralds represented the 'Pillar of Fire' and was called Joachim, which signifies inauguration or establishment.

When interpreted Qabbalistically, the names of the two pillars mean 'In strength shall My House be established.' When the High Priest stood between the pillars as a mute witness to the perfect virtue of equilibrium he personified the divine nature of humankind in the midst of our egocentric nature. On one side towered the awesome column of the intellect; on the other, the brazen pillar of the flesh.

Just as the subconscious and conscious natures of our mind are married and joined by our super-consciousness (*Logoic Consciousness*), so these two pillars as ONE symbolize the pinnacle of our spiritual evolutionary journey in a physical body. That journey is symbolized in the legacy of, and forces identified with, the twin pillars.

The pillar of Boaz in the Biblical story and in Masonry symbolizes the animating aspect of Source, the Source's vital energy in creation. The Pillar of Joachin not only represents our intellect, but also our concrete, physical, earthly nature.

MetaSpiritually, the two pillars could signify our left and right brain hemispheres. That implies Boaz could be symbolic of the right hemisphere which is associated with the intuitive, abstract, and creative energies. And Joachim could represent our left hemisphere which is associated with logic and the intellect. The pillars could also represent our nervous system which has three main parts: the central nervous system (brain and spinal cord), the middle pillar; the peripheral nervous system (all body nerves that lie outside of the central nervous system); and the autonomic nervous system (controls our involuntary actions) which represents the third pillar.

Tzedakahic Practice

Tzedakah comes from the Hebrew and means 'an obligation to fairness' or 'righteousness.' It refers to the religious obligation to do what is right and just, regardless of your financial standing. It's synonymous with the Islamic term *sadaqah* which means 'voluntary charity.' So, I invite you to, by all means, step up your *tzedakahic* tendencies.

ॐ   ॐ   ॐ

Unblurring

Unblurring is taking your materialistic blinders off so you can see the spiritual landscape around you.

Undiscovered Consciousness

Once the undiscovered consciousness level of higher spiritual awareness is reached, local and nonlocal universal and galactic connections become the same thing as far as function. There's no labeling, no sense of separation, no apartness. There's stillness because there is only Universal Beingness! Wholeness just is. Oneness is the only form of expression. You will discover that omnipresence, omnipotence, omniscience and omni-activity just are!

Undiscovered consciousness operates at 'speeds' that we might describe as speeds a gazillion times faster than those generated by Lilliputian consciousness through *'quantum ether.'* Since super-luminal *(super-nonlocal)* interactions exist, they are 'nonlocal' in the sense of nonphysical, instantaneous connectedness (which is itself a misnomer, because there would be nothing to be connected since that implies a differentiation that doesn't exist). Quantum information is *'received'* before it's *'sent'* (which is also a misnomer because everything at this level of being just is—all at once)! Essentially, this level of Pure Universal Beingness is Absolute Unbounded Meta-Oneness (AUM). (See OM Oomph reference.)

Unholy Instants

Anytime you have inclinations toward divinity-denying concepts and ideas, false judgments, poor choices and/or actions, you experience unholy instants of a perceived separation in consciousness of your True Divine Nature.

Unicorn Mythology

The unicorn myth has very deep metaphysical roots. The interpretation I resonate the most with is its relationship to our pineal gland. The horn, emanating from the unicorn's forehead implies the existence of the mystical pineal Third Eye which replaced the boney horn. According to the ancient hidden wisdom traditions, the unicorn's spinal cord was presumed to extend beyond the *medulla oblongata,* and protrude through the pituitary gland and then out of the forehead between the eyes. This horn-to-inner eye mythology implies that our exteriorly-focused physical senses, when developed to their highest spiritual essences, metamorphosize into there psychic counterparts. In this case, the pineal enhancement morphs into clairvoyance (clear extrasensory perception). (See ᵀʰᵉThird Eye and Five Physical Senses references.)

Universe

Science and religion talk about different universes—religion through the filter of dogma and science through the eyes of empirical research.

Universal Substance

The presence of Universal Substance (the Infinite Field) is inexhaustible because everything is made of it. The Infinite Field can continually meet your needs in countless seen and unseen ways because It's the ground of all manifestation as well as the unmanifest. Choose to stay in alignment (oneing) with your Divine Nature, sharing, giving generously, and accepting gratefully whenever and wherever you are.

Unified Field

Quantum physicists are searching for a unified field that holds all of the answers to the mysteries of the universe 'out there.' While I'm very interested in their quantumly defined unified field, I'm also just as interested in another Unified Field – the union between our human nature and our Divine Nature.

Unity's Tawhidic Nature

Tawhidic unity is a mystical experience that means experiencing your oneness with the Eternal Presence. *Tawhid* is the Arabic doctrine of your oneness with God. It not only means seeing your oneness with the Source of All, but '*feeeeeeling*' your indivisibility and wholeness with the Infinite Isness. *Tawhidic* unity is more than knowing about your divine connection, it's experiencing that cosmic connection first hand. You accomplish this through meditation, affirmative prayer, a multiplicity of spiritual practices, and right living. You feel a sense of what's rarely attainable in the midst of a busy, multi-faceted modern life.

Unitary Mystical Experiences

Unitary mystical experiences are not simply monitored by neurological testing which appears to reduce these transcendent experiences to a flurry of neural blips on SPECT scans. The monitors only register (record) the brain areas affected by these anomalous mystical experiences and cannot gage how much these experiences transform the mystic's consciousness. The brain is the mind's somatic recorder (filter) and 'collects' these experiences, placing them in our memory banks and archiving them for future reference. This suggests that the brain's neuroplasticity is our triptych to higher states of consciousness.

Unity

Unity is not the same thing as uniformity. One of unity's benchmarks is diversity. Uniformity prides itself in breeding sameness.

There'll come a time when there'll be a total and complete entrainment of your egocentric consciousness with your super-consciousness, so there's universal harmony and unity. When that happens, the totality of your residual impurities and a multitude of repressed materialistic attachments will be exorcised from your consciousness. When that happens you'll operate consciously at a higher order of being.

Universe

There's no dividing line between the universe and you, because you are the universe expressing itself as you through the *Logoic Vibration (Spanda* pulse*)*. (See *Spanda* reference in *More Straight Talk* book.)

As far as we know the physical universe is the lowest, most dense, vibration of the One Universal Presence. And since there are many levels (facets, dimensions, vibrations) of the One Presence in physicality the differences between these levels are more vibrational than spatial.

Just as, in quantum physics, without an observer, there's no universe—without our *Logoic Self (Divine Self, Universal Divine Nature, Higher Spiritual Self)* there would be no human 'universe.'

Unquestioned Answers

Most people are comfortable with unquestioned answers. It means they don't have to think their way out of them.

Unself-Consciousness

It's your insperiences and mindful experiences that help you achieve the unself-consciousness that leads to your *Self-Consciousness*.

Upskilling

Spiritual growth and unfoldment, from atom to sun, are based on the voltage of your soul's urge for enlightenment and wholeness. Your skin school experience has limitations, but not as many as you might think! Because you are a spiritual being having a human experience there are things—plenty of things—you can do to expand your awareness by upskilling your esoteric knowledge and experiential depth so you can enjoy being Home. Higher thought is a lifelong endeavor. It requires an open mind and a desire to comprehend deeper truths. Upskilling your spiritual perspective places you at the cutting edge of human thought. It moves you past the limitations associated with concrete operational thought and the relative realm to allegorical and metaphorical thinking and the Absolute realm.

Use Your Inside Voice

How many times have you heard a parent whisper to a child, "Shhhh. Use your inside voice?" How many times have you said that to your own children or grandchildren? Just prior to that warning the youngster is usually speaking at a pitch louder than is deemed necessary. The idea is you want the youngster to learn proper etiquette and accepted behavior.

But the 'inside voice' I'm referring to is a different kind of 'inside voice.' It's a voice we must learn to listen to when we're facing difficulties, when we suffer major setbacks, when we run into ten miles of bad road. It's a voice we must listen to if we are to grow personally and professionally. It's a voice we must pay attention to if we are to master the art of living. It's the voice that comes from what psychologists refer to as our *Authentic* or *True Self.* It's the 'voice of inner strength.' It's the 'Still Small Voice.'

When the world is screaming its woes—when friends are letting you down—when you want to yell out in frustration and pain—when you're experiencing a dark night of the soul moment —that's when the ONLY thing to do is … Use Your Inside Voice!

ॐ   ॐ   ॐ

Vertical Farming

Try a little vertical farming to deepen your spirituality. That means seeking highly advanced spiritual teachings (skyscrapers). In an agricultural context, vertical farming is the practice of cultivating crops on the balconies and rooftops of skyscrapers. The higher teachings (skyscrapers) Cher and I are prescribing are considerably beyond your normal spiritual 'reads.' For example, some of the best 'vertical farming' you will ever do are reads like: Helena Blavatsky's *Secret Doctrine*, and her *Isis Unveiled*; J.J. Hurtak's *The Keys of Enoch*; Geoffrey Hodson's *The Hidden Wisdom in the Holy Bible*; Baruch Spinoza's *Ethics*; Corrine Heline's *New Age Bible Interpretation,* and her *The Mystery of the Christos*; I.K. Taimni's *Man, God and the Universe*; Emma Curtis Hopkins' *Mental Practice*; Hans-Werner Schroeder's *The Cosmic Christ*; Ram Das' *Be Here Now.*

Others include Annic Besant's *Esoteric Christianity;* Alice Bailey's *Esoteric Psychology*; Matthew Fox's *The Coming of the Cosmic Christ*; Benjamin Creame's *Maitreya's Mission;* Rudolf Steiner's *The Philosophy of Spiritual Activity;* Charles Leadbeater's

Astral Plane and *Devachanic Plane*; John Shelby Spong's *Biblical Literalism: A Gentile Heresy*; Annie Besant and Charles Leadbeater's *Talks on the Path of Occultism*; Christopher Hills' *Nuclear Evolution*; Dora Van Gelder's *Devic Counsciouness;* Jiddu Krishnamurti's *The First and Last Freedom.*

But wait! I've got more: Bart Ehrman's *Misquoting Jesus* and *Jesus Before the Gospels*; and our very own verse-by-verse *New Metaphysical Versions of all Four Gospels*, selected passages from all of the New Testament books, and the verse-by-verse metaphysical interpretation of the *Book of Revelation: A Manual Describing the Unfoldment of Our Christ Nature*, also (of course) *Rev. Bil Unplugged and Unedited* that you're reading now! As you can see, this is serious 'vertical farming.' These higher thought 'skyscrapers' will deepen your spirituality and put you well on the path of enlightenment.

Vibhutic Practice

Vibhuti is sacred ash which is made of burnt, dried wood used in Hindu Agamic rituals that are composed of readings from cosmological, epistemological, philosophical doctrines, precepts on meditation and practices, and four kinds of yoga. The rituals teach a system of spirituality involving ritual worship and ethical personal conduct. The sacred ash is smeared across the forehead as a consecration of the practice. In another, more esoteric sense *'vibhutic ash'* could stand for our sacred cremains when we ritualistically leave our physical bodies after another earth experience. As a soul growth 'practice' it could refer to our repeated reincarnations.

Virtues

Even if you're not giving full expression to kindness, compassion, forgiveness, authentegrity, unconditional love, joy, superior intuition, wisdom, generosity, and non-judgmentalness—know they're the innate qualities of your True Spiritual Nature—and can be expressed and developed if you choose to do so.

Vows

It's much better to take a vow of silence than risk voicing a set of vowels that cause harm to relationships and interfere with someone's spiritual growth.

ॐ   ॐ   ॐ

Walking on Water

The story of Yeshua (Jesus) walking on water (controlling the nature of water), according to the literal account (Matthew 14), tells how he demonstrated his power over water by not sinking into its depths. A similar 'power over water story' was supposedly demonstrated by Moses who parted the Red Sea. So, it seems as if Jesus is not only being pitched as having supernatural powers like Moses, but even being superior to Moses because of his messianic qualities.

MetaSpiritually speaking, 'walking on water' means mastering the negative experiences of life and turning them into positive, life-affirming growth experiences.

Walking Your Talk

Cher and I consider it a privilege to walk the MetaSpiritual path on loving, kind, compassionate, faithful, intuitive, lotus-inspired, Self-Realized feet.

Mother Teresa said that "If there were poor on the moon, she'd go there." Cher and I feel the same way about people the world over who don't realize that they are the One Reality (Pure Universal Consciousness) expressing Itself through the Cosmic Logos in human form as them. We'll go to the ends of the earth to share that universal Truth.

*When it comes to walking our talk,
we prefer backbone to wishbone!*

Whatness

The 'what' (*quiddity*) of a thing is based on a scholastic philosophical reference taken from the Medieval Latin *quidditas* which means 'essence' or the 'whatness' of a thing.' I believe the physical (planetary, galactic, quantum) 'Whatness' (Essence) of the Pure Universal Consciousness (God, One Reality, etc.) is the Cosmic Logos in all of Its atomic and subatomic forms (expressions). (See *Cosmic Logos* and *Spanda* references.)

When Push Comes to Shove

There's a hand exercise Cher uses our workshops to make a point when push comes to shove. It's 'I' opening, so I'm going to pitch it to you: Put your hands in the prayer position. Okay, now push your right hand against the left. What's your left hand doing? Pushing back! Ever had that happen in life? Someone pushes against you, and what do you do? Push back. What do they do? Push harder! It's a no-win situation. But what if you didn't resist? Go ahead, push with your right hand without resisting with your left. Wow! Movement happens! The same happens in life. When we stop pushing – when we stop trying to MAKE things happen, but instead open ourselves up to the inflow of Divine Ideas and the guidance of our intuition and common sense, it's incredible how much easier life becomes.

Where Did Cain Get His Wife?

Where did Cain get his wife during his restless wandering in the Land of Nod in the Hebrew Testament story? You won't find the answer in the 'Land of the Literalbots.' The answer to that perennial question is in the 'Realm of Allegory.'

According to the literal account in the *Book of Jubilees*, Cain married his sister Awan who bore his first son, the first Enoch,* reportedly 196 years after the creation of Adam. Cain then establishes the first city (presumably Tenoch), naming it after his son, Enoch. Cain builds a house, and lives there until it collapses on him, killing him. Let's take a quick MetaSpiritual look at this allegory. You already know what Cain represents. (See Land of Nod reference). Awan symbolizes the addiction to materiality. The *first* Enoch, the product of their union signifies the intellectual pursuit of worldly pleasures. What this story is telling us is that our unabashed pursuit (constantly living in) of worldliness which comes from a sense-addicted consciousness (build a house) will continue to implode (collapse) any tendencies we may have toward our spiritual growth and reinforce the abject denial of our innate divinity (kill us). (*The second Enoch was the son of Jared and father of Methuselah. Genesis 5: 18-24.)

Wholeness

Cher and I use scientific research from many disciplines—neuroscience, quantum physics, psychoneuroimmunology aepigenetics, and evolutionary biology, to name a few—to accent, expand and deepen our spirituality. And this truckload of research suggests—no confirms—that nature's fundamental drive is not hard-wired competitiveness, as we were taught years ago, but unitive WHOLENESS. And we believe it's that urge toward wholeness that will lead us—you, humankind—into a fully self-actualized and *Self-Realized* spiritual being in no matter what dimension of being we happen to inhabit.

Whore of Babylon

The Whore of Babylon is also called the Scarlet Harlot). Her full title is given as 'Babylon the Great, the Mother of Prostitutes and Abominations of the Earth.' The word 'whore' can also be translated metaphorically as 'idolatress.' Within fundamental Christian eschatology the whore and beast are anthropomorphized. However, from a MetaSpiritual standpoint the supposed 'whore' is not a woman at all and I consider the uncouth reference to a woman's sexual status as a typical patriarchal indignity! Both the 'whore' and the beast refer to our sense-addicted, divinity-denying, unenlightened egocentric nature which lays with monstrous, self-aggrandizing thoughts every chance it gets.

Why the Resurrected Jesus Visited Hell

According to the literal interpretation of Genesis 6:1-2, and 4 when: 'There were giants in the earth in those days; and… when the Sons of god' saw the daughters of men that they were fair… they took them wives who were from the daughters of Cain.' These 'sons of god (Brahma)' were demonic demigods who were reported to exist at the dawn of pre-human history. They were called Rakshasas whose chief pastime was seducing the human race. What's interesting is that in the apocryphal book of *The Acts of Pilate* and C.G. Harrison's *The Transcendental Universe,* the Rakshasas that were left continued to influence human desires until the time when the *Cosmic Logos* incarnated as Jesus of Nazareth. According to the authors of 1 Peter 3:18-20 and Ephesians 4:9 the *Cosmic Logos* as Jesus "descended into the forecourts of Hell (Sheol) in order to preach to those who were disobedient."

It's believed that it wasn't human beings the *Cosmic Logos* as Jesus met in hell, but disembodied Rakshasas! This subterranean act was the banishment of the enemies of humankind which has its echo in the saga of the Antichrist implied in the Book of Revelation. His descent into Sheol proved that the effects of the Rakshasas can be nullified once and for all. And it's that perspective that's the basis for the following MetaSpiritual interpretation which makes it clear that we have the power to nullify any and all divinity-denying thoughts, words and actions (our Rakshasa tendencies) that we allow to delay, derail and/or block our Self- Realization: This Vedic Rakshasas myth, coupled with its subsequent interpretations throughout the centuries, reminds us of the power of myths as metaphors for our evolving spiritual growth.

When we devote ourselves to our spiritual development by conscientiously aligning our human self with our *Cosmic Logoic Self (Higher Spiritual Self)*, we have the power to nullify the seductive sensory addictions of our hypocritical, cannibalistic, and highly materialistic egocentric nature (Sheol) so we can achieve the *Self-Realization (Cosmic Logoic purity)* that's ours by right of consciousness.

Widdershins Perspective

A *widdershins* religious perspective is a 'counterclockwise' belief in an anthropomorphic god meme 'out there' separate from us, instead of believing our *Cosmic Logoic Nature* (our *Higher Spiritual Self*) vibrates as us. The Oxford English Dictionary's entry cites the earliest uses of the word from 1513, where it was found in the phrase '*widdersyns* start my hair (my hair stood on end).

Willpower

How many times have you begun with zeal and excitement, because your faith was strong, and you were filled with confidence and enthusiasm? But then you didn't see instant results, and you questioned the process. This is when the power of your spiritually-attuned WILL keeps you going, and brings with it the dawn of a new, higher level of understanding. You're able to continue moving forward in your process of ever expanding spiritual awareness. During this process it's important to note that your will and your understanding are working together. You can't make wise choices if you don't have the spiritual understanding to inspire more elevated decisions. Key point—here's what you can KNOW: The manifestation of what you Divinely Order is, without exception, far greater than anything your unenlightened human ego could envision, and it never comes at the expense of another person.

"Wizdom"

Devoted spiritual study, disciplined meditation and right living will turn your evolving wisdom into *wizdom*, because connecting with the proverbial 'Still Small Voice' accelerates your deeper awareness and thus the wisdom (*vidya*) you can share at a moment's notice (in a *wiz!*). By the way, in my opinion, the 'Voice' isn't still or small. It's dynamic and expansive because It's your entire *Cosmic Logos Nature* trying to get your attention!

The **Word**

The Word, *logos* (Greek) and *dabhar* (Aramaic), does not mean 'word' as we understand it linguistically. It's God (the One Reality, the Infinite Isness, the Eternal Presence, our Cosmic Logoic Nature) as physicality. It's the 'Word made flesh,' the subtle creative pulse of the unmanifest Universal Substance (as *Spanda,* the *Cosmic Logos*) manifesting into dynamic living forms. It's an inter-dimensional and intra-dimensional creative pulse (cosmic vibration). Without the 'Word' (*Spanda*) there would be no physical universe. (See the *Cosmic Logos* reference in this book; and the *Arche, Apeiron,* and *Spanda* references in our *More Straight Talk About Spiritual Stuff* book.)

Work

Cher's and my message to people in unfulfilling work is that work isn't a static end point or even merely an exercise in putting food and bread on the table. It's a lifelong pilgrimage in which the human, flesh-and-blood you is tested, refined, deepened, and transformed in the world of business. In work as in life, people must be willing to do the right thing. And the *right thing* is to be courageous enough to express your *SuperSelf*™ because your Divine Nature is your only saving grace. Your conscious alignment with your *SuperSelf*™ will keep you centered and prosperous in whatever work you choose to do and give you the courage to keep your power, status, and position in perspective.

When the spiritual work you do sheds light,
occasionally you'll get burned by those
who want to live in the dark.

World Hunger

World hunger is not caused by a scarcity of food, but by a scarcity of loving and compassionate brotherhood and sisterhood.

World of Outer Appearances

How many times have you heard the assertion, "Perception is reality?" You've no doubt heard that statement many times before. Perception, however, may not be a reality! Perception is only perception. It creates a reaction which may or may not be grounded in fact. Many of the assumptions we make every day are based on our familiarity with the world around us so we see what we expect to see and nothing else. You must learn to look past the obvious. That is, look beyond the familiar. The more you choose to expand your experiential horizons the better your chances of seeing big, important, unfamiliar 'things' *out there* in the world of appearances.

World Peace

It will be a great day when spiritual communities and churches get all of the money they need and the armed services have to hold bake sales and bazaars to purchase bombers, tanks, aircraft carriers, surface to air missiles, and mortars. Better yet, what if there would be no need for military armaments at all!

Sharing our light spiritually is amazing, and it truly does make a difference. But perhaps the best way to make a difference and contribute to the peace we all want to see is to share our light one-on-one, on a day-to-day basis. World peace is a noble dream—but how can we have world peace if we don't have peace within our family, with our neighbors, in our meetings or at work ... if we don't have peace within ourselves! That peace begins when we share our special, unique light with others, connecting with one another to rekindle the human spirit, and grow a powerful light of love and truth throughout the world.

Peace on earth has been derailed by grace scarcity, compassion scarcity, unconditional love scarcity, kindness scarcity, inclusiveness scarcity, forgiveness scarcity, and so on. Piecemeal caring needs to be amped up quite a bit, don't you think?

World Spiritual and Religious Banners and Flags

Cher and I have a collection of world Interfaith, multifaith and esoteric spiritual and religious banners and flags, including the gorgeous OM Lotus Banner, which is our favorite. But we don't have a white flag! We'll never surrender our open-mindedness, and in particular, our MetaSpiritual perspective which is defined by it.

World Soul

The Planetary *Logos* (the *Incarnate Cosmic Logos,* God as physicality) is the World Soul crucified on the cross of matter. It'll continue Its sacrifice until humankind achieves conscious Self-Realization in our universe and other intelligent beings achieve a similar awareness in their dimensions of being.

World Spirituality

Cher and I are affirming a world that is post wars and violence, post child abuse, post denigration of women, post hunger, post materialistic, post religious fundamentalism and Biblical literalism, post religious founder and/or guru worship, post anthropomorphic god worship, post Gaia abuse, post cultural and nationality prejudices, post doing harm to anyone, post bigotry, post animal cruelty, post religious exclusivity, post injustice, post racism and sexism, post narrow-mindedness, post dogmatism, etc.

Worthship

When you worship an anthropomorphic 'God meme out there,' you cease to see your own divine *worthship* and the innate divine worthiness in other people that can bring you and everyone else closer to *Self-Realization.*

Don't believe anyone who tells you that you aren't worthy. You are worthy because you are directly associated with your Higher Spiritual Self. That means your *worthship* is guaranteed, because by nature you're a divine being who has chosen a human experience. It's in your spiritual DNA!

You, as much as anyone in the entire cosmos, deserves love, respect, compassion, affection, confidence, wisdom and sense of worthship. Why? Because your worth is already in your DNA. It's guaranteed by your innate Divinity, which is your *Cosmic Logos Nature.* (See the teases about *Spanda* in the Trinity, Universe and Word references in this book and the *Spanda* reference in our book entitled *More Straight Talk About Spiritual Stuff.*)

Fear, shame and guilt are the three major emotional barriers to feeling a sense of worthiness, and fundamental religious organizations religiously 'retail' all three negative emotions.

Worthship is actually derived from the Old English word 'woerthship.' The two roots, 'worth' and 'ship,' tell us a lot about what worthship is according to Cher's and my expanded definition of *worthship.* 'Worth' is pretty obvious, it means 'equivalent value or distinction, congruent parity, of the same quality.' 'Ship' in Old English it means 'to shape, to configure, to fashion or mold.' So, in terms of our value and worth as spiritual beings having a human experience, our worthiness (*worthshipness*) is due to our distinctive value as human expressions of the *Cosmic Logos* which has shaped (molded, fashioned) our *True Nature (Higher Spiritual Self)* in Its distinct, congruent equivalent image.

You'll never be completely comfortable or at peace with yourself without your own approval.

There's no need—absolutely no need—to worship an external deity to seek its approval or protection. You came into this earth experience already divine! You are a priceless spiritual being clothed in a human body. Your considerable worth is in your DNA. Don't believe anyone who tells you differently.

Undervaluing who you are is dissing your innate divinity. It's blaspheming against your *True Self,* the *Cosmic Logos* expressing Itself as you in human form!

You don't have to hustle for worthiness. You don't have to bargain for it or jump through hoops to for it. Simply accept your worthship. You've been worthy, valuable, priceless and precious since you were born into this human experience—and before. Why? Because you are a spiritual being having a human experience which is underwritten by the *Cosmic Logos* which is expressing Itself in human form as you!

The Cosmic Logos which has incarnated as you has set the standard for your worthiness because It's the Universal Perfect Standard.

The fact that we may be flawed humans doesn't negate our incredible worthship. Our human blemishes are like the block of granite that covers the priceless statue within. When we chip away at our shortcomings on our way to aligning our human self with our Logos Nature, we'll uncover the Real Us, the Extraordinary Us, our Higher Spiritual Self. There's already a masterpiece within us, our Logos Nature!

Just so I'm clear, you're already worthy by right of consciousness. MetaSpiritually, 'consciousness' stands for 'house,' and there are many 'mansions' (states of human awareness) in the Pure Universal Consciousness (House). Pure Universal Consciousness is the only 'House.' There's no 'repent mansion,' or 'reprehensible mansion,' or 'wretched mansion,' or 'pathetic mansion,' or 'worthless mansion,' or 'pitiful mansion' when it comes to the value of a human being. All of these 'mansions' are human inventions, created to diminish someone's self-worth and self-esteem according to the motives and whims of our egocentric nature. They do not define us, only bind us, if we let them.

Your self-worth is not so much what people say it is, it's what you choose to answer to—and won't answer to—that indicates how much you know about your value.

Please don't let your understanding of your divine *worthship* as a human expression of the *Cosmic Logos* embarrass you. Your 'deification' has nothing to do with ego narcissism. It has everything to do with your *True Divine Nature*. Your divine worthship was guaranteed when the *Cosmic Logos* incarnated as you when you first arrived in skin school.

Wuxing

Wuxing is the fivefold-elemental change theory of the period of growth through the period of rest in Chinese philosophy. By analogy it bears a loose resemblance to the Seven Days of Creation in Jewish and Christian mythology. It's also known as the Five Elements, Five Agents, Five Processes, Five Stages, Five Steps, Five Phases, Five Virtues and Five Planets. Its five elements are: wood, fire, earth, metal and water. The *wuxing* system describes the dynamics of natural phenomena and extends to the description of aesthetic principles, historical events, political structures, and social norms. *Wuxing* has developed into a conceptual device that is used to explain not only cosmology, morality, and medicine, but virtually every aspect of Chinese life and thought.

ॐ   ॐ   ॐ

Xenoglossia

I'm under the impression that *xenoglossia* occurs when we speak a mysterious language that we could not have acquired through studying that language. It's a paranormal occurrence that may very well come from our having connected psychically with another version of us in another dimension of being. (See our *Quantum Self* reference.)

ॐ   ॐ   ॐ

Youology

If you've ever been a bad commercial for the Real You, reverse that trend.

You're positively, absolutely the most qualified person on the planet to be yourself. You can be yourself any time you want. You can be beside yourself if you want, although Cher and I don't recommend your doing that too often. You can be behind yourself or get ahead of yourself. You can know yourself or "no" yourself by running from yourself. One thing we know for sure about you —it becomes you to become you.

Your 'Calling'

Those who think they must do only what they've been trained to do, told they're qualified to do, or forced to believe they can only do—and then settle for it—have made a choice to abandon their special purpose in life. I recommend your doing what gives you energy and fulfillment. Do what brings you joy and a sense of completeness—something that brings you inner peace – something that helps make the world a better place for everyone. That special inner prompting may or may not mean you'll ever have a six-figure income. But it'll mean something much more than that – it'll mean you're doing what your heart-centered inner voice has led you to do. It'll mean you've found your *Authentic Spiritual Self.* (See Inner Prompting reference.)

ॐ   ॐ   ॐ

Zen There's You

The only Zen you find on silent retreats, meditation insperiences, vision quests, mountaintop experiences, and Om pod sessions is the Zen you bring with you.

It's better to be Zenful than 'sinful.' Wouldn't you agree!

To practice Zen and the art of improved Christian motorcycle maintenance, do the following: All owner's manuals feature a chart listing the maintenance tasks which describes what needs to be done. Typically, these tasks are identified with the letters: I, C, R, A, and L, which respectively stand for Inspect, Clean, Replace, Adjust and Lubricate.

> *It's okay if you want to be a little Zen in your texting or in your emails—just avoid any attachments.*

In spiritual growth terms, that means you must *inspect* your current understanding of your true spiritual, not religious, nature; *clean* up your language by deleting any reference to any type of anthropomorphic 'god out there'; *replace* all dogma with a more metaphysical and scientific mindset; *adjust* your human personality to be more in alignment (oneing) with your *Higher Spiritual Self;* and *lubricate* your body with natural, anti-inflammatory, antioxidant, and antimicrobial healing oils and moisturizers instead of chemical-laden products.

ॐ ॐ ॐ

INDEX

About the Author:

Rev. Dr. Bil Holton has been writing, speaking, coaching, and publishing for over 30 years. As a Spiritual Thought Leader, ordained Unity minister, 21st Century metaphysician, and student of science and spirituality, Rev. Bil has a solid reputation for his strength of character, engaging personality, out-of-the-box thinking, and strong work ethic. His extraordinary metaphysical teachings and his ability to bring spiritual Truths into clarity by combining science and spirituality put him in high demand as a teacher and spiritual coach.

When he isn't involved in neuroscience research, studies in quantum physics, and metaphysical writing, Bil enjoys golf, travel, ballroom dancing, jigsaw puzzles, the theatre, and landscaping.

Rev. Bil, together with his wife and business partner, Rev. Cher Holton, founded The Global Center for Spirital Awakening, with a mission to help pepoplemaster the art of "living in skin school" by walking the spiritual path on practical feet.

Revs. Bil and Cher bring a strong background to their spiritual work, through their corporate business, The Holton Consulting Group, Inc., founded in 1982. They have worked with clients in the U.S., Canada, Germany, England, and South America, with a mission of leading, guiding, and inspiring people and organizations to live productively and joyfully at the speed of life ... one choice at a time.

On a personal note:

Bil and Cher take what they call "Indiana Jones Experiences" including white-water rafting, sky-diving, helicopter fly-bys and even fire walking to push their risk-taking envelopes. But one of their most exciting adventures led them into the world of ballroom dancing, and they are amateur student couple champions in several ballroom dance categories. They even have a ballroom dance floor in their home!

The Holtons have six grandchildren who live close to them, and provide Bil and Cher many opportunities to bond with them ... and then give them back to their parents! (That's what grandparents do—right?)

You might be interested in exploring other spiritually-oriented books by Rev. Dr. Bil Holton:

The Gospel of Matthew, New Metaphysical Version
The Gospel of Mark, New Metaphysical Version
The Gospel of Luke, New Metaphysical Version
The Gospel of John, New Metaphysical Version
The Book of Revelation, New Metaphysical Version
Spiritually Speaking: A Metaphysical Interpretation of Spiritual, Religious, and Modern Day Secular Terms (for those who are more spiritual than religious)*
Reconciling the Church's Science Phobia: The Dance Between Science and Spirituality*
Straight Talk About Spiritual Stuff*
Power Up Your Life! Accessing Your Twelve Powers to Achieve Health, Happiness, Abundance, & Inner Peace*
Crackerjack Choices: 200 of the Best Choices You Will Ever Make*
Right Thoughts, Right Choices, Right Actions: 200 of the Best Choices Unity People Will Ever Make*
Business Prayers for Millenium Managers*
Get Over It! The Truth About What You Know That Just Ain't So**
Get Over These, Too! More Truth About What You Know That Just Ain't So!**

* Co-authored with Rev. Dr. Cher Holton
** Co-authored with Rev. Dr. Paul Hasselbeck

ॐ   ॐ   ॐ

Ordering/Speaking Information:

To order copies of Dr. Holton's books,
and request information about scheduling him
for speaking engagements, visit his website at
http://www.TheGlobalCenterforSpiritualAwakening.com
or contact his office at 919.767.9620.

www.ingramcontent.com/pod-product-compliance
Lightning Source LLC
Chambersburg PA
CBHW061757110426
42742CB00012BB/1920

* 9 7 8 1 8 9 3 0 9 5 8 6 1 *